ADB Foreword

Economic progress in Asia and the Pacific has been remarkable in recent decades, but there has been a price to pay: the region has become the world's leading source of greenhouse gas emissions. In fact, Southeast Asia region is one of the most vulnerable in the world to climate impacts, as changing climate has affected communities, infrastructure, food security, and the well-being of its people. This scenario has worsened due to the coronavirus disease (COVID-19) pandemic.

The Asian Development Bank (ADB) estimates that $1.7 trillion per year is needed to support climate resilient infrastructure in developing Asia. Members of the Association for Southeast Asian Nations (ASEAN) need $120 billion per year, but face an estimated annual funding gap of over $100 billion as of 2021. Indonesia alone needs $74 billion per year, with an annual financing gap of $51 billion. To bridge the infrastructure funding gap, private investment needs to be scaled up. National and regional infrastructure plans play a key role in economic growth and social development, but recovery and investment strategies of the region must not undermine achievements made in reducing dependency on fossil fuels and protecting the environment.

Indonesia has the potential to pursue a green recovery; this report shows that only 4% of the total stimulus funding has been allocated towards the green sector. To increase this percentage, Indonesia should prioritize green spending and reallocate fiscal spending from fossil fuel intensive sectors toward green and sustainable assets, projects, and expenditures. The pursuit of climate goals does not need to constrain economic achievements, but offers an opportunity for sustainable growth. For example, ADB has calculated that a $172 billion investment in five low-carbon and green sectors (sustainable urban transport, clean energy transition, circular economy, agriculture, and oceans) could create up to 30 million direct jobs in Southeast Asia by 2030. Indonesia can capture much of this potential.

Indonesia is committed to delivering its Nationally Determined Contribution goal of reducing carbon emissions by 29% by 2030—41% with international finance support—and ADB remains committed to supporting the Government of Indonesia and other developing members in achieving goals to reduce climate change. ADB was the first multilateral development bank to set clear climate investment targets for 2030 in its Strategy: ADB first committed in 2015 to increase its climate investments to $6 billion annually by 2020; a target it met in 2019. ADB raised its ambition to deliver $100 billion in cumulative financing between 2019 and 2030 to combat climate change, including $34 billion in cumulative adaptation and resilience investments, and $66 billion for mitigation.

In particular, ADB launched two of the most innovative initiatives for Southeast Asia during the United Nations Climate Change Conference of the Parties (COP26) in November 2021 in Glasgow, UK: (i) the ADB Energy Transition Mechanism partnership (ETM), which will leverage a market-based approach to accelerate the transition from fossil fuels to clean energy; and (ii) the ASEAN Green Recovery Platform, with total pledges of $665 million managed by ADB to mobilize an additional $7 billion for low-carbon and climate-resilient infrastructure projects in Southeast Asia, and accelerate green recovery from the pandemic in the region. In Indonesia, ADB has been working closely with PT SMI and the Ministry of Finance in developing a Green Finance Facility under the national SDG Indonesia One Platform to support the achievement of sustainable development goals (SDGs) for Indonesia through an innovative transition financing mechanism. ADB has approved a $150 million loan in 2022 to provide funds for subprojects that meet green, financial bankability, and leverage targets with the aim of catalyzing funds from private, institutional, and commercial sources.

ADB is working with governments across Asia and the Pacific to address financing shortfall by supporting strategies that catalyze green finance from both the public and private sectors, and has intensified its efforts since 2020 to expand access to green and sustainable finance through the development of capital markets in the region.

ADB is proud to support this important and timely report—through technical assistance from the ASEAN Catalytic Green Finance Facility (ACGF)—as part of a longstanding relationship with Climate Bonds Initiative (Climate Bonds) in the region. ADB and Climate Bonds will continue to work together to grow green finance markets in Indonesia and the wider region and seek to meet the common goals of a prosperous region and a sustainable planet.

Ramesh Subramaniam
Director General, Southeast Asia Department,
Asian Development Bank

ACGF Foreword

Accelerating Green Finance for a Post-COVID-19 Recovery in Southeast Asia

The United Nations Climate Change Conference of the Parties (COP26) held in Glasgow in November 2021 highlighted two things. First, the planet was not on course to achieve its needed targets for limiting global warming to below 2°C (preferably 1.5°C) as agreed by most countries in the Paris Agreement in 2015— "a code red for humanity" per the UN Secretary General. Second, there were encouraging initiatives that emerged and needed to be scaled up and mainstreamed quickly.

Looking at Southeast Asia, the key to a real impact on climate change efforts is rapidly scaling up capital flows especially from private capital sources—banks, bonds, funds, public–private partnerships—into green projects. The region needs around USD210 billion a year for climate resilient infrastructure until 2030, and in many sectors the financing gap reaches 50% or more. Indonesia's own annual climate-adjusted infrastructure financing needs between 2016 and 2020 were estimated at $74 billion on average, with an annual infrastructure financing gap of USD51 billion, according to the Asian Development Bank (ADB).[2] To meet these financing gaps, large infrastructure projects need support for (i) transitioning to bankability; (ii) accessing private capital, with innovative and green financing models; and (iii) rapidly scaling up the models across sectors.

The ASEAN Catalytic Green Finance facility (ACGF) is a key solution to the challenges listed above that were discussed at COP26 in Glasgow, where the Green Recovery Platform for the ASEAN region was also launched.[3] With more than $2 billion in funds including technical assistance grants, the ACGF has been focusing on creating de-risking and innovative green finance mechanisms such as the SDG Indonesia One Green Finance Facility, encouraging capacity development on green and innovative finance models and frameworks, and focusing on relatively untouched thematic areas such as the Blue SEA Finance Hub launched from ADB's Jakarta office in 2021, among other activities. Additionally, ACGF's work on supporting green, social, and sustainable bonds has already led to very successful issuances in Thailand, and it is being expanded further in the region.

Building green finance mechanisms, capacities, and models must go hand in hand with national road maps for green finance and crucially green project pipelines. The ACGF has been working with CBI on the Green Infrastructure Investment Opportunities (GIIO) series of reports, which brings together several of these facets into a national context. We are confident that the GIIO Indonesia 2022 Report will be of immense benefit to catalyzing the needed projects and capital flows for accelerating the country's climate change ambitions and targets.

Anouj Mehta
Unit Head ACGF and Country Director
Thailand Resident Mission, Southeast Asia Department,
Asian Development Bank

PT Sarana Multi Infrastruktur (PT SMI) Foreword

Indonesia is committed to take part in combatting climate change and this is shown through the country's commitment in the Paris Agreement to reduce greenhouse gases. It is targeted that greenhouse gases will be reduced by 29% through the country's own capacity and 41% through international support by 2030. In this regard, PT Sarana Multi Infrastruktur (Persero) ("PT SMI") with the support of Ministry of Finance Republic of Indonesia has shown its concrete action such as issuing the first corporate green bond in Indonesian capital market in 2018 and also establishing the SDG Indonesia One platform, which aims to further accelerate infrastructure development that bolsters sustainable development goals by being a platform to provide support from public and private sector to projects using blended finance scheme.

Indonesia still faces some challenges to bolster the development of green infrastructure, as shown by the wide climate and infrastructure financing gap. Green finance could be one of the best options to this, with various financing instruments and funding sources that can be catalyzed to close the climate and infrastructure financing gap. Through SDG Indonesia One platform, PT SMI is able to help facilitate mobilization of private capital and public funds in a blended finance framework and channel these funds to projects that helps to further the agenda of mitigating climate change, which also advances the achievement sustainable development goals.

Another challenge to the development of green infrastructure in Indonesia is presented in infrastructure bankability. Currently, this is being addressed through de-risking mechanisms and providing technical assistance, where blended finance schemes also help to facilitate these needs. PT SMI has been taking a big role in implementing blended finance schemes, among other various innovations to support green infrastructure.

There is ample green infrastructure pipeline in Indonesia and the need for support in the sector should be addressed. The investment requirement to achieve the 2025 renewable energy mix target is massive and there lies the needs of private funds to be mobilized. This shows that blended finance schemes, green bonds and other innovations are needed to answer the challenge and PT SMI is committed to help solve the gaps in the sector.

Under G20 Indonesia Presidency, sustainable finance become one of the main topics. It is hoped that by using this very good momentum, more stakeholders would be willing to participate in contributing into the development of green infrastructure. The first step to this is through raising awareness and the Green Infrastructure Investment Opportunities Indonesia Report can help in further advancing this agenda. Not only that, it is also expected that the report could also in turn help to attract capital flow towards the green sector, as it presents various insights on the needs and gaps of green infrastructure and shows ample opportunities for green investments in Indonesia.

Edwin Syahruzad
President Director, PT Sarana
Multi Infrastruktur (Persero)
Jakarta, January 2022

1. Green infrastructure presents an opportunity for growth: Introduction to this report

Introduction

Green infrastructure presents a huge investment opportunity in Indonesia, especially in energy and transportation. It is estimated that Indonesia requires USD322.8bn worth of climate compatible infrastructure and climate assets by 2030, in which energy and transportation make up around 75% of Indonesia climate funding needs at USD245bn.[4]

The effects of climate change and the risks associated with a greater than 2°C rise in global temperatures by the end of the century are significant: rising sea levels; increased frequency and severity of hurricanes, droughts, wildfires, and typhoons; and changes in agricultural patterns and yields.

Investment in low-carbon solutions will be essential for meeting global emission reduction pathways under the Paris Climate Change Agreement.

Since 2019, there was an increasing demand from institutional investors—particularly from OECD nations and China—for investment opportunities that address environmental challenges and support sustainable development. Institutional investors and banks manage assets worth over USD120tnn that could be used for infrastructure investment.

Growing interest from investors in green projects has resulted in the development and growth of innovative financial products. The global green bond market has grown rapidly, cumulative total labelled issuance stood at USD2.1tn at end H1 2021; cumulative green issuance at USD1.3tn.[5]

Green finance needs to scale up much further to achieve global climate targets and infrastructure needs. This report builds on the inaugural *Green Infrastructure Investment Opportunities Indonesia* reports released in May 2018 and December 2019. It provides updated content to help meet the growing demand for green investment opportunities in Indonesia—including green bonds—and informs the transition of the country to a low-carbon economy.

The report is intended for a wide range of domestic and regional stakeholders including policy makers, project development bodies, regional institutional investors, asset managers, and infrastructure groups, as well as government ministries (Finance, National Development Planning, Energy and Mineral Resources, Transportation, Environment and Forestry).

The Nationally Determined Contribution of Indonesia under the Paris Agreement

Reduction in annual greenhouse gas (GHG) emissions:
29% below 2010 levels by 2030, and up to 41% with international support.

Methodology

This report considers four key sectors that are considered to be traditional infrastructure assets, low-carbon, and generate climate positive impacts: renewable energy, low-carbon transport, sustainable water management, and sustainable waste management. Green energy and transportation are emphasised as they will have the highest funding needs by 2030. The Climate Bonds Taxonomy is used to identify which projects and assets are green.

Case studies have been used to show the types of opportunities available in the short- and medium-term future. The green credentials, funding options, status, financial structures, and possible investment pathways are explored for each case study.

The transport, water, and waste projects have been drawn from the government pipeline of National Strategic Projects, as outlined by the Committee for the Acceleration of Priority Infrastructure Delivery, as well as from the latest government list of external loans 2020–2024. Projects are chosen based on their national significance as identified by the Government of Indonesia.

There are various ways for an investor to gain exposure to a specific project, asset, or portfolio. The possible investment pathways will vary depending on the asset ownership structure, the stage in the financing lifecycle of the asset, and the mandate of the investor. Projects with public and private funding may also differ.

This report features two case studies per sector. A more comprehensive list of green projects from public pipelines is available in Annex II: Sample Green Pipeline.

"Transformation towards new and renewable energy as well as acceleration of green technology-based economy will become a crucial transformation in our economy."

President Joko Widodo[6]

"Climate change is a global disaster that will have a greater magnitude than the COVID-19 pandemic. Like COVID-19, no countries can escape from the impacts of climate change. Which is why countries around the world are racing to mitigate the catastrophic impacts of climate change."

Sri Mulyani Indrawati, Minister of Finance[7]

2. Green recovery and sustainable finance trends and opportunities

Indonesia is the largest economy in Southeast Asia and among the fastest growing emerging market in the world. Even though the coronavirus disease (COVID-19) pandemic dampened economic prospects for Indonesia in 2020, the country recovered from the recession in the second quarter of 2021. The president set out "green" as one of the key economic growth strategies.[8] A recovery stimulus that prioritises spending on green and climate infrastructure can be a vehicle for Indonesia to achieve a more resilient economy and realise its vision of green economic growth. This can be achieved by prioritising investments in climate infrastructure and nurturing a supportive regulatory framework that can unlock global green capital.

Quality infrastructure is known to be the driver of economic growth and underpins broader economic and industrial activity. Infrastructure also plays a key role in bridging gaps in the United Nations Sustainable Development Goals (SDGs). Under the Joko Widodo administration, infrastructure has been a national priority and the country has made considerable strides in infrastructure spending. During 2015–2021, infrastructure spending almost doubled from IDR256.1tn (USD17.9bn) in 2015 to IDR408.2tn (USD28.6bn) in 2021.[9] 2021 held a record high for infrastructure spending. For the first time in 6 years, infrastructure spending exceeded IDR400tn.[10]

Even with such remarkable spending growth, Indonesia is still facing infrastructure gaps. Infrastructure stock—particularly in connectivity—has not been able to keep up with the rising demand.[11] This is contributing to the fall of Indonesia in infrastructure rankings such as the IMD World Competitiveness Ranking, from 53rd in 2019 to 55th in 2020.[12] Physical assets including hard infrastructure are also facing challenges from growing exposure to environmental risk from disasters and climate change.

Climate disasters such as extreme weather events, floods, droughts, sea-level rise, and weather variability have been disrupting the population and causing substantial economic loss. For example, the cost from the Jakarta 2020 flood was estimated to be at IDR5.2tn (USD360m).[13] Climate disasters also come at a heavy social cost. Approximately 1.2 million residents on the north coast of Java have been frequently affected by severe coastal and tidal flooding.[14] Such climate disasters are only expected to intensify in the future which calls for much more resilient and adaptive infrastructure. It is predicted that without proper adaptation infrastructure, 4.2 million people could be exposed to permanent flooding by 2070–2100.[15]

Threats from climate risks and disasters require current and future infrastructure to be built to withstand expected climate shocks.[16] Indonesia is committed to delivering its Nationally Determined Contribution (NDC) goal of reducing 29% carbon emissions by 2030, 41% with international finance support. To meet this, it requires an investment of USD322.8bn (IDR4,520tn) by 2030 for mitigation. A large part of the solution is scaling up investments in green infrastructure especially in clean energy and sustainable transport.

Pandemic posed a unique challenge

The coronavirus disease (COVID-19) pandemic brought countries globally into recession, and Indonesia experienced a 2.1% GDP contraction in 2020.[17] Even though the contraction was considered modest compared to ASEAN counterparts, the social costs such as poverty and job loss were severe. The Minister of Labor estimated that from February 2020 to February 2021, roughly 1.62 million Indonesians lost their jobs, and 15.72 million workers were forced to reduce work hours.[18] From March 2020 to March 2021, 1.12 million people had fallen into poverty, increasing the rate of poverty from 9.78% to 10.14% in that same period.[19]

Indonesia rolled out massive stimulus funding under the National Economic Recovery (PEN) programme for emergency relief and to support economic activities. The stimulus funds were largely spent on healthcare, social programmes, and state-owned stimulus. The PEN programme prevented heavier social loss from the pandemic.[20] A massive vaccination programme is largely underpinning the economic recovery of Indonesia. The government is planning to continue this in 2022 through an increased 2022 healthcare budget. Healthcare—mainly dedicated to vaccination—will account for 9.2% of budget allocation in 2022, up from 6.2% in 2021.[21]

As the economy recovers, reflected as 3.5% GDP growth in 2021, Indonesia will need to plan a longer term growth strategy, paving the way for a sustainable post-COVID-19 recovery.[22]

Indonesia can recover better, and greener

As economic recovery starts to emerge, Indonesian stimulus will have to focus on longer term recovery planning. This means reviving economic activities to the level they were before the pandemic by addressing economic challenges—such as job loss—and ensuring that the economy will be resilient to future disasters such as climate shocks. The stimulus is prioritised to spur labour intensive industries such as housing and manufacturing to create new employment post pandemic.[23]

Similar to the crisis brought by the pandemic, the climate crisis has been recognised as a crisis with equal if not greater enormity.[24] The economy needs to become more resilient to climate disasters, and future stimulus spending must be targeted at climate-smart assets and infrastructure.

Indonesia has the potential to pursue a green recovery as it has only allocated 4% of the total stimulus funding towards the green sector.[25] This percentage should be increased in the next round of fiscal stimulus. Indonesia could prioritise green spending and reallocate fiscal spending from fossil fuel-intensive sectors towards green and sustainable assets, projects, and expenditures. Pursuing a climate goal does not need to be done at the expense of economic achievements. For example, the Asian Development Bank (ADB) calculated that a USD172bn investment in five low-carbon and green sectors (sustainable urban transport, clean energy transition, circular economy, agriculture and oceans) could create up to 30 million direct jobs in Southeast Asia by 2030.[26] International Finance Corporation (IFC) analysis shows that investments in selected green sectors could create 213.4 milllion cumulative new direct jobs during 2020–2030.[27]

Ensuring adequate green investment for a sustainable future is an economic imperative as much as it is an environmental one. Climate disasters are recognised to have destabilising long-term impacts on the financial system.[28] Without enough climate risk mitigation, financial risks such as borrower default, credit risk, and stress on insurers are more likely to happen.[29] A green recovery could be the first step towards the green economic vision of Indonesia and safeguard the economy from future climate shocks. It would also put Indonesia on a resilient economic growth pathway, making the post pandemic economic recovery more sustainable.

Mobilising private capital is critical to close the climate and infrastructure funding gap

Spending adjustments were made by the government to address the more urgent pandemic and healthcare spending. In 2020–2021, the government increased the pandemic fiscal response package from 3.8% to 4.9%.[30] This created a fiscal space constraint for other sectors including infrastructure and climate.

The Indonesia state budget alone has not been enough to close the infrastructure funding gap. According to the Medium-Term National Development Plan (RPJMN), Indonesia requires an IDR6,444tn (USD451bn) of infrastructure financing during 2020–2024 and the state budget would only be able to meet 37% of this.[31] The rest of the funding will need to be met by state-owned enterprises (SOEs) and the private sector.

Figure 1: Indonesia's Infrastructure Financing Framework 2020–2024

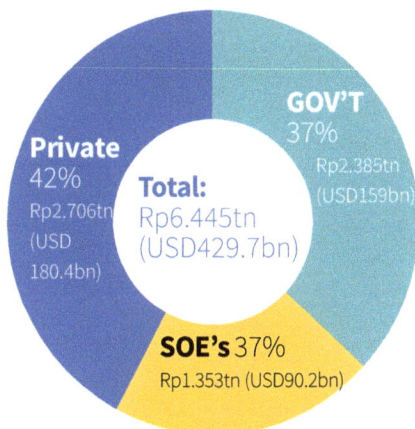

GOV'T 37%
Rp2.385tn (USD159bn)

Private 42%
Rp2.706tn (USD 180.4bn)

Total: Rp6.445tn (USD429.7bn)

SOE's 37%
Rp1.353tn (USD90.2bn)

Source: Source: Ministry of Housing and Public Works

The Ministry of Finance has reiterated its commitment to sustain climate spending, but even before the pandemic the climate funding gap was wide. It is estimated that Indonesia requires USD322.86bn (IDR4,520tn) to meet its emission target by 2030.[32] During 2016–2020, the Indonesia state budget on average had only been able to meet 34% of these funding needs.[33]

As the state budget is insufficient, private and international finance will be critical for Indonesia to close its climate and infrastructure funding gaps.

ASEAN is increasingly appealing to investors

Emerging markets (EM)—such as in ASEAN countries and including Indonesia—are increasingly appealing to investors. Several foreign entities—including development banks as well as foreign commercial banks—have issued green bonds in local ASEAN currencies demonstrating interest in domestic markets. Other green bond issuers such as BNP Paribas, Société Générale, Bank of America, and the National Australia Bank have issued vanilla bonds,(unlabelled conventional bonds) in at least one of the local ASEAN currencies. Issuance

in local currencies allows foreign issuers to tap domestic investors for capital. Interest in ASEAN markets continues to grow.

Global green finance demand is growing

There is strong global green finance momentum. At the 2021 United Nations Climate Change Conference (COP26), the Glasgow Finacial Alliance for Net Zero committed to over USD130tn of private capital to transform the economy to net zero. The number of commitments and allocation of capital to green assets trends in an upward trajectory. The number of global funds linked to Environmental Social and Governance (ESG) doubled from 2019 to 2020.[34] However, during 2013–2017, the total capital allocation towards green assets by large pension funds increased from 2.6% to 7.5%.[35] These increases were seen across asset classes such as green bonds, green equity indexes, and other green assets (endnote 33).

> "In recent years there has been significantly more engagement from institutional investors for integrating ESG in their investment process [in ASEAN] and the wealth management industry is now following."
>
> **Valentin Laiseca,**
> Head of ASEAN Index Sales, MSCI[46]

> "We have some very long-term horizons. If you're a long-term investor, you can focus on specific areas, like Southeast Asia funds... [where] there is a source of growth."
>
> **Ted Lee,** Senior Portfolio Manager, Canadian Pension Plan Investment Board[47]

Box 1: Climate Bonds *Green Bond European Investor Survey* shows interest in EM.

The Climate Bonds Green Bond European Investor Survey asked respondents to describe their appetite for emerging market (EM) green bonds and to outline what they could be receptive to buying. Most respondents (82%) could buy EM debt, with exposure limits at country and issuer level tending to apply more to respondents that have a greater degree of integration of green bonds. However, the most common restrictions are credit rating (69%), currency (65%), and deal size (58%).

As most respondents could—and would—like to buy EM green bonds, EM issuers must consider how these requirements can be reconciled. Respondents expressed that they would like to increase their holdings in EM sovereigns. Countries such as Indonesia (two bonds in US dollars), Seychelles (US dollars), and Lithuania (Euros) have issued green bonds which met with a positive reception from investors

Three-quarters of respondents able to buy EM green bonds treated EM differently from developed market green bonds, stating that they required more evidence of integrity to invest in green bonds from EMs. Respondents also ranked factors that could make investing in EM green bonds more attractive and bring scale to the market. Respondents most frequently selected the option of credit enhancements available from multilateral and/or public entities, with more than half considering it important or very important.

Respondents listed the following features as giving them more confidence to invest in EM green bonds:

i. Transparency, e.g. adherence to GBP, reporting Use of Proceeds (65%);

ii. Reliability, e.g. external reviews (Second Party Opinion, audit, certification, etc.) (48%); and

iii. Risk, e.g. insurance/Credit Default Swaps(CDS)/guarantees, size of the issue, currency (25%).

More information on this topic can be found in the Green Bond European Investor Survey, on the Climate Bonds Initiative website.

Green labelled debt instruments are an effective means of directing investment capital towards climate change mitigation and climate change resilience and adaptation projects, including green infrastructure. Growing interest from investors in green projects has resulted in the development and growth of innovative financial products including green, social, and sustainability (GSS) bonds and loans; and green index products.

As of 2021, green bonds are the most developed segment of thematic instruments, with broader acceptance from the investor base. Globally, the volume of green bond and loan issuance has risen sharply from USD171bn in 2018 to USD269.5bn in 2020, USD5bn in 2018 to USD 29.4bn in 2020 for ASEAN cumulative issuance, buoyed by strong interest from both investors and issuers.[36]

Investor demand in Indonesia can be seen from the rising number of impact and sustainable investors participating in sovereign green *sukuks*. Sukuk is defined as an Islamic/Shari'ah compliant bond.[37] Sovereign green *sukuks* saw growing interest from green investors during 2019–2020. The allocations to investors describing themselves as green increased from 29% in 2019 to 35% in 2020. In 2021, the number doubled to 57%.[38]

Green financial instruments can be used to attract and tap into global green capital, and Indonesia is already well-positioned to do so, as evidenced by the numerous government policies and initiatives driving green finance. The market saw multiple GSS labelled bond issuances during 2018–2021.

Sustainable Finance Overview in Indonesia

Indonesia is already developing its green bond market infrastructure, as evidenced by the surge of green and sustainability bonds during 2018 – 2021 and the emergence of a green taxonomy. 2021 also saw the announcement of green and sustainability bonds from major SOEs, such as PLN and Pertamina.[39] The sovereign green bonds have driven the development of the market. As of 2021, the Indonesia Ministry of Finance had issued eight green and sustainable bonds.

Table 1: Indonesia Green, Social, and Sustainability Bond Market Overview[48]

As of November 2021, the Indonesia GSS bond market stood at USD7.7bn, with green bonds contributing USD6.3bn to the total. 17 GSS bonds have originated from Indonesia.[49] 2021 saw three new sovereign bonds and the first-ever sovereign SDG. Other issuer types included financial corporates and banks (PT SMI, Bank BRI), and non-financial corporates (Star Energy Geothermal and Tropical Landscape Finance Facility). Star Energy Geothermal is the only repeat non-financial corporate issuer from Indonesia.

Proceeds were allocated to a wide range of mostly state-owned green infrastructure projects across Indonesia including renewable energy, low carbon transportation, sustainable waste management, and sustainable water infrastructure such as flood control infrastructure.

As of 2021, there have been eight sovereign GSS *sukuks* and bonds from Indonesia, with a total volume of USD4.9bn. Indonesia issued the first global green *sukuk* in 2018, and the first green retail *sukuk* in 2019. 51% of the proceeds refinanced existing projects, and 49% financed new projects.

Investor demand also included interest from retailers. The IDR5.4bn (USD378m) sovereign green retail *sukuk* issued in 2020 attracted 16,992 retail investors, up from only 7,735 retail investors involved in the November 2019 bond issuance.

The USD2.5bn triple tranche *sukuk* issued in June 2020 to accommodate the pandemic response had a 5–year tenor. The USD750m green tranches were oversubscribed by 7.73 times, with proceeds allocated to finance and refinance green projects. In June 2021, the ministry also issued a USD3bn triple tranche sukuk which included a 30–year, USD750m green tranche, the longest green sukuk to date.

The expected green taxonomy will help to attract green capital

To enable green finance and green bonds, Otoritas Jasa Keuangan (OJK) published a sustainable finance roadmap in 2014, and OJK Regulation No. 51/ POJK.03/2017 in 2017. The roadmap marks the starting point for the sustainable finance 10–year plan of Indonesia, which included plans for the implementation of a green taxonomy. The regulation is an umbrella regulation for all rules on sustainable finance—including regulating a green bond—and provides a basic guideline for the green bond issuance process.

A taxonomy can increase and direct the flow of global green capital into the domestic market and can be used as a tool that ensures that investments will be channelled into the right SDG and climate assets. On 20 January 2022, OJK released the first edition of the Indonesia Green Taxonomy. Following extensive analysis of over 2,700 sectors and sub-sectors, 919 were included in the Green Taxonomy with accompanying eligibility requirements. Indonesia has taken a different approach to the taxonomies of China, EU, and others by designing a traffic light system for each activity where green represents business activities that protect, restore, and improve the quality of environmental protection and management, as well as climate change mitigation and adaptation...', yellow represents practices that do no significant harm, and red represents harmful activities.

While other jurisdictions have talked conceptually of a traffic light system, this is the first taxonomy where this approach has been detailed. Most of the activities have three sets of criteria: green, yellow and red. Around 94 activities, including some activities in the mining and extractive industries sector, have no green criteria, therefore are not considered as green. The taxonomy does not specify different environmental objectives with all environmental objectives addressed through the same set of criteria.

Climate Bonds has yet to undertake a full review of the taxonomy against international equivalents, but an initial review indicates that while there are some departures from international equivalents which may challenge its interoperability, it is a credible starting point and a useful contribution to the taxonomy landscape. This taxonomy is only the first edition, therefore it will be important that the next iteration of this taxonomy aligns with internationally acceptable standards, such as the Common Ground Taxonomy published by the International Platform on Sustainable Finance. This will ensure cohesion between domestic and international market participants.

To encourage a sector sustainability transformation and increase company transparency, OJK has asked all financial institutions and public companies to submit a sustainable finance action plan and a sustainability report by April 2022.[40]

Table 2: List of Indonesian Green, Social, and Sustainability Bonds

Green bonds

Issuer name	Amount issued	Issue date	Use of Proceeds
Republic of Indonesia (green retail sukuk)	Rp5tn (USD350m)	Nov 2021	Energy, Waste, Water
Republic of Indonesia (global green sukuk)	USD 750m	Jun 2021	Energy, Waste, Water
Republic of Indonesia (green retail sukuk)	Rp5.4tn (USD378m)	Dec 2020	Energy, Waste, Water
Star Energy Geothermal (Darajat II) Ltd	USD320m	Oct 2020	Energy
Star Energy Geothermal (Darajat II) Ltd	USD790m	Oct 2020	Energy
Republic of Indonesia	USD 750m	Jun 2020	Energy, Waste, Water
Republic of Indonesia (green retail sukuk)	Rp1.4tn (USD98m)	Nov 2019	Energy, Waste, Water
Republic of Indonesia	USD750m	Feb 2019	Energy, Waste, Water
OCBC NISP	USD150m	Aug 2018	Energy, Transport, Water
PT Sarana Multi Infrastruktur (SMI)	USD35th	Jul 2018	Transport, Energy, Waste, Water, Land Use
Star Energy Geothermal (Wayang Windu) Ltd	USD580m	Apr 2018	Energy
Republic of Indonesia (global green sukuk)	USD1.25bn	Mar 2018	Energy, Waste, Water
Tropical Landscape Finance Facility I Pte	USD96m	Feb 2018	Land use
Total	**USD6.3bn**		

Sustainability bonds

Issuer name	Amount issued	Issue date
Republic of Indonesia (SDG Bond)	€500m (USD573m)	Sep 2021
PT Indonesia Infrastructure Finance	USD150m	Jan 2021
Bank Mandiri	USD300m	Apr 2021
Bank Rakyat Indonesia	USD500m	Mar 2019
Total	**USD1.5bn**	

The green bond market infrastructure in Indonesia is developing but is at an early stage. Some issuers still face challenges with the issuance process, especially during pre- and post-issuance. The lack of domestic expertise—such as verifiers and external reviewers—can add challenges for first time issuers.[41] Such challenges are shared by other EM GSS debt markets but can be actively addressed.

The required infrastructure such as second party opinion (SPO) providers, verifiers, and green bond impact reporting advisory firms is not well developed in nascent green bond markets like Indonesia. As of end of 2021, issuers still rely on international organisations and SDG centres in local universities to support their pre- and post-issuance processes. This makes green bond issuance complicated and could elevate costs for local and new issuers.[42] Green bonds of smaller sizes (< USD100m) incur costs that are relatively high compared to loan financing.[43] Issuers also have to meet the costs of establishing credibility, such as obtaining a second party opinion or green certification, which can be discouraging.[44]

These elements should be important considerations when designing mechanisms to strengthen the green bond market ecosystem. Incentives such as meeting the administrative cost for a green bond issuer—like the grant scheme set by the Monetary Authority of Singapore—were not available in the Indonesian market in 2021.[45] Introducing a grant or subsidy scheme would send a strong signal for potential GSS bond issuers and encourage new issuers to enter the market.

Other initiatives and policies facilitating green infrastructure and finance

The pillars of the Indonesia climate and transition financing strategies are the Climate Change Fiscal Framework, Energy Transition Mechanism, Disaster and Climate Pooling Fund, and carbon pricing scheme. Indonesia has several dedicated green or sustainability funding pooling available, such as the Environmental Fund Management Agency—widely known as BPDLH—and SDG Indonesia One (SIO). More examples of green financing instruments in Annex I.

Previous actions (up to December 2019)	New and planned actions (since 2019)
No regulations on carbon pricing.	The Ministry of Finance introduced a carbon tax, effective April 2022. Regulations for carbon trading are under development.
The government developed the Roadmap for Sustainable Finance in Indonesia 2015–2019, to achieve sustainable development through comprehensive support of the financial service industry.	OJK is drafting a green taxonomy as a part of the Roadmap for Sustainable Finance Phase II.
The Ministry of Finance launched a climate finance tracking and reporting system and undertook a green budget tagging exercise with support from UNDP.	The Ministry of Finance created a broader financing framework to include other labelled debt products such as sustainability and social bond, signalling interest to issue more sustainability-labelled bonds in the future.
Indonesia incorporates low-carbon economic development into its Medium-Term National Development Plan 2020–2024 (RPJMN 2020–2024), through the Low Carbon Development Initiative (LCDI) roadmap.[50]	Indonesia sets a Net-Zero target by 2060 and coal phaseout by 2056.[51]
	Launched a partnership with ADB to carry out Energy Transition Mechanism.[52] This mechanism will buy out coal plants to enable coal plants to be retired earlier.
The government created a Green Bond and Green Sukuk Framework for sovereign bonds and has issued two sovereign green sukuk.	The Ministry of Finance has issued a green-tranche global sukuk to finance COVID-19 recovery. The Ministry of Finance has issued four green sovereign sukuks and a global SDG bond since 2019.
The Financial Service Authority developed a regulation on the Issuance and Terms of Green Bonds. Domestic green bonds are required to comply with it and encouraged to adopt the ASEAN Green Bond Standards.[53]	The Ministry of Finance has broadened the scope of its green financing framework to include social and sustainability projects, setting the ground for future issuance of wider labelled bonds.[54]
Indonesia established the Environmental Fund Management Agency—widely known as Badan Pengelola Dana Lingkungan (BPDLH)—a mechanism to distribute green funds towards environmental projects.	
The government removed barriers to and undertook reform for developing/investing in infrastructure, including: • Reforms for streamlining approval and procurement procedures for infrastructure projects. • Removal of the withholding tax on interest payments in foreign currency denominated government bonds.[55] • Opening direct lending from multilateral organisations to SOEs. • Improvements to the government public–private partnership (PPP) regulations for infrastructure, the provision of subsidies for PPPs, and credit enhancement for PPPs and SOEs in the form of sovereign guarantees, gap viability funding, and availability payments.[56]	The Indonesian government launched: • The Upgraded Online Single Submission licensing system. This expedites the issuance of licensing and simplifies the investment procedure. • 19 special economic zones (SEZ) as of 2021. Aimed to attract investment, develop new infrastructure, and spur economic growth in less developed areas.
The government developed the Indonesian Internal Credit Rating scorecard system and the Indonesia Infrastructure Guarantee Fund (IIGF) for administering sovereign guarantees. It also created specialised agencies, some including: • The Investment Coordinating Board of Indonesia (BKPM), a centralised service, is responsible for issuing more simplified foreign investment licences. • The Committee for Acceleration of Priority Infrastructure Delivery, established as a coordinating unit to streamline national infrastructure project management, in line with National Strategic Projects and Priority Projects.	
PT SMI was the only state-owned enterprise (SOE) that issued a green bond in 2018.	PLN and PERTAMINA—the two largest SOEs in electricity utilities and oil—are planning to issue a green or sustainability bond to finance their renewable portfolio.[57] In partnership with ADB, PLN has since launched a Sustainable Finance Framework in November 2021.[58] Pertamina is establishing an ESG framework.
Indonesia joined the Sustainable Banking Network (SBN)	Minister of Finance Sri Mulyani Indrawati was elected as one of the Co-Chairs of the 2021-2023 Coalition of Finance Ministers for Climate Action in 2021.

Source: Indonesia Green Infrastructure Investment Opportunities, 2019 Indonesia Update Report (Updated)

Other barriers to infrastructure financing and green bond issuance

Before an infrastructure project can successfully access private capital or issue a debt instrument, the project first needs to be bankable and align with the risk appetite of institutional investors. Due to the unique infrastructure cash-flow profile, large scale infrastructure projects typically have varying and upfront high risks that the private sector is either unable or unwilling to assume. Public institutions or development finance institutions (DFIs) typically will step in to provide the necessary de-risking instruments to unlock private finance.

The bankability of the infrastructure pipeline is still cited as a main challenge in attracting earlier private finance into an infrastructure project. Problems around bankability can vary but among the most common is the limited capacity for project owners in meeting project preparation standards. Some green infrastructure projects have not met investor standards. The readiness of municipal and local government project owners is also a barrier to the growth of a green municipal bond market.[59]

Low capacity and unreliable off-takers remain common challenges faced by renewable energy and water projects in Indonesia.[60] Public sector or multinational institutions typically step in to provide revenue guarantees or other de-risking instruments, however improvements to government capacity and regulatory reform are still required to dissolve these barriers.

Green bonds also carry risks including those of liquidity and/or currency. Liquidity allows for more accurate and consistent pricing of new bonds in the primary market. The Indonesian market for debt securities and sukuks is relatively illiquid due to its small overall size. Higher liquidity in secondary markets would have a positive impact on the development of the market as a whole, and pricing of new bonds in the primary market will become easier.[61] To achieve this, more benchmark sized (bond of at least USD500m equivalent) from a diverse range of issuers are needed. Currency risk pertains to exchange rate fluctuations that affect the value of an investment or—in the case of a bond issuer— alter the cost of bond repayments. Indonesian issuers bringing bonds in foreign currency typically require an accompanying intervention to mitigate currency risk.[62]

Barriers like project risks and bankability have been preventing issuers from accessing private capital through green bonds, so addressing these barriers and risks will be important for Indonesia to increase the scale in the market. The public sector and DFIs can step in to lower these risks through de-risking and other project facilitating instruments, like guarantees or technical assistance for project preparation.

Role of Development Finance Institutions

Indonesia benefits from the support of domestic and multilateral DFIs such as ADB, the Asian Infrastructure Investment Bank (AIIB), KfW (Kreditanstalt für Wiederaufbau), Agence Française de Développement (AFD), Islamic Development Bank, World Bank, and PT Sarana Multi Infrastruktur (PT SMI). These DFIs have a two-fold role in mobilising private capital towards green infrastructure projects. First, DFIs can spur green bond market creation through anchor investing, market facilitation and capacity building. Second, DFIs can reduce the high-risk and high upfront costs from an early state green infrastructure project. These two activities can help to lower the barriers to private capital involvement in the market.

DFIs have been acting as market facilitators for nascent green bond markets in ASEAN and Indonesia by issuing local currency bonds. This creates liquidity and issuance in local economies. For example, the IFC issued a green bond in June 2018 in Philippine pesos (a Mabuhay bond) and one in Indonesian rupiah (a Komodo bond) in October 2018. PT SMI also issued the first corporate and rupiah-denominated green bond for Indonesia in 2018. Multilateral banks like IFC and World Bank can also subscribe to private placements or be anchor investors in debt issuance and initial public offerings to help entities gain investor confidence and catalyse investments from a wider pool of private capital. [63] IFC, for example, invested in the OCBC NISP Tbk USD150m green bond in 2018.[64]

Through deals like these, DFIs have supported market creation by participating in first-time issuances and helping create more visibility for new issuers among the investment community. This in turn establishes pricing points, encouraging issuers to return to market publicly and paving the way for other prospective issuers. [65] Investors like repeat issuers, particularly from EM. Not only does company due diligence not have to be repeated, but a track record of transparency and trust can be established and leveraged by the issuer.

DFIs have a crucial role in facilitating green projects to be more bankable and investable through offering de-risking instruments and providing technical assistance during project preparation. This financial and capacity building support can provide confidence and attract institutional investors to fund green infrastructure.[66] DFIs can achieve this by offering blended finance schemes, credit enhancement mechanisms, and de-risking instruments such as viability gap funding, first-loss provisions, contingent and A/B loans; overall, they reduce risk exposure and enhance market incentives for investors.

Blended finance schemes have been gaining importance in Indonesia due to their relevance for large scale infrastructure projects. Globally, the blended finance model is seen as an innovative approach to attract private capital.[67] A successfully blended finance scheme can generate more bankable project pipelines through de-risking and technical support, and would ultimately contribute to lowering credit risk and enabling private finance flows into the project.[68]

Finally, DFIs can act as a platform to attract private capital and catalyse investments from a wider pool of private actors (both international and domestic). For example, ADB launched the ASEAN Catalytic Green Finance Facility (ACGF) under the ASEAN Infrastructure Fund (AIF), an initiative to mobilise over USD2bn from cofinanciers such as as AFD, KfW, the European Union, or the Foreign, Commonwealth & Development Office (FCDO) of the United Kingdom, among others, for green infrastructure in Southeast Asia by supporting governments in the region prepare and finance infrastructure projects that promote environmental sustainability and contribute to climate change goals.[69] Nationally, Indonesia has the SDG Indonesia One (SIO) platform launched by the Ministry of Finance in 2018 and managed by PT SMI. SIO, a financing platform dedicated to accelerating achievement of the SDGs, is aimed at mobilising and channelling funds from various sources— including private, philanthropic, and development partner—to sustainable infrastructure projects.

Box 2: Sustainable Development Goals Indonesia One

The Ministry of Finance and PT SMI launched SDG Indonesia One (SIO) in 2018. This platform aims to scale up existing sustainable infrastructure projects through financing and co-financing, de-risking, project development facility, equity investment, and capturing private and commercial funds to accelerate the achievement of SDGs in Indonesia. In 2021, PT SMI is also introducing a green finance facility, a de-risking facility that will link funds provision to subprojects with clear green objectives. The implementation of this facility is supported by a sovereign financial intermediary loan from ADB.[70] SIO also serves as a facilitator between global investors and domestic sustainable infrastructure projects.

As of 2021, SIO had successfully pooled USD3.24bn from diverse sources of funding; philanthropy, bilateral donor, climate funds, multilateral, commercial banks, sovereign wealth funds and institutional investors.[71] The platform has channelled USD231m to sustainable infrastructure projects such as renewable energy, waste management, and water supply and sanitation projects.[72] It has also committed to supporting USD790m of sustainable infrastructure projects, supported the preparation of 49 projects, and financed seven sustainable infrastructure projects.[73]

SIO was created to address two main barriers for green infrastructure investments in Indonesia: The infrastructure funding gap, and the lack of bankable green infrastructure projects. SIO can contribute to scaling up green infrastructure projects by offering products that can support projects from during project identification, project preparation, project structuring, development and operation, and monitoring and evaluation. These products are classified into three categories:

i. Development facilities. Increasing the overall quality of the project pipeline, this platform offers technical assistance to project owners during pre-feasibility studies. Facilities offered are in the form of policy, framework and regulation support, capacity building, research activity on thematic topics, providing bankable feasibility study, technical assistance, review feasibility study and project documentation.

ii. De-risking facilities. Mechanisms such as credit enhancement instruments, investment premium schemes, and geothermal resource risk mitigation.

iii. Financing and equity. Mobilising private financing by allocating and pooling funding from private banks or commercial funds and providing and facilitating equity to strengthen the capital capacity for new (greenfield) projects and help recycle assets for already operating projects (brownfield)

The SIO platform has supported numerous programmes that create an enabling environment, some of which include capacity building and business case studies to improve sector reform and invite private participation. SIO has supported projects during project preparation, such as solar rooftops in seven airports in Indonesia. SIO has also provided project structuring support for Gresik Regional Water Company (PDAM), SPAM Dumai, and others. SIO has also provided project financing for the Padang Guci 2 Minihydro Powerplant and Deli Serdang Biomass Powerplant, among others.

These mechanisms are accessible to state-owned, local, and national infrastructure projects owners.

PT SMI also played a key role in disbursing government stimulus to regional governments and other SOEs. When National Economic Recovery (PEN) programme funds prioritise green infrastructure, SIO could contribute to kickstarting a post COVID-19 green stimulus.

"One of the objectives for the establishment of SDG Indonesia One is to become a blended finance platform that could invite many international partners such as donor, philanthropy, climate fund, DFIs/MDB and Institutional Investor. It will accelerate our effort for the transition to low-carbon economy and also contribute to the post-pandemic economic recovery and the achievement of SDG in Indonesia".

Edwin Syahruzad,
President Director PT SMI (Persero)

Source: PT Sarana Multi Infrastruktur

Box 3: ASEAN Catalytic Green Finance Facility

Launched in April 2019 under the Association of Southeast Asian Nations (ASEAN) Infrastructure Fund (AIF), the ASEAN Catalytic Green Finance Facility (ACGF) signifies ASEAN member country commitment to promote sustainable infrastructure development and address climate change in the region. It is the only regionally owned green finance initiative focused on developing and scaling up climate projects among member states of ASEAN. As of 2021, ACGF has committed to supporting around USD500m for nine projects, with a total portfolio of nearly USD3bn.

The ACGF offers loans and technical assistance to support governments in identifying and preparing commercially viable green infrastructure projects. ACGF loans provided from AIF equity can be utilised to cover upfront capital investment costs, while regional technical assistance—supported by ADB technical assistance resources and grants from development partners—supports project structuring and origination activities. This two-pronged approach de-risks green infrastructure projects, making them more attractive to private capital investors.[74]

ACGF has also partnered with SDG Indonesia One and recently prepared underlying subprojects for a financing facility for green infrastructure projects. This will be a financial intermediation loan from ADB to the Republic of Indonesia, to be relent to PT SMI, to implement the Sustainable Development Goals Indonesia One–Green Finance Facility (SIO-GFF) project. A pipeline of approximately USD423m has been identified. ADB's USD150m SIO-GFF loan will provide funds for subprojects that meet green, financial bankability, and leverage targets with the aim of catalyzing funds from private, institutional, and commercial sources. SIO GFF will ensure availability of funds for an evolving pipeline of green and SDG-impacting infrastructure projects and de-risking.[75]

ACGF could further support post COVID-19 green stimulus by channelling technical assistance support for developing de-risking mechanisms, on a country-by-country basis.[76] For instance:

i. Insurance against specific risks, first-loss provisions, purchasing equity, or mezzanine tranches of securitised bonds.

ii. Support for the issuance of tailored structures, such as zero-coupon bonds designed to avoid interest during the economic re-building in the coming five years (2021 – 2025), or step-up coupons with a similar objective.

iii. Support for the development of asset-backed structures that would allow off balance sheet re-financing of sustainable assets and ease pressure on constrained public sector balance sheets.

These mechanisms could also be available to qualifying bond issuance programmes from banks, municipalities, and private companies. To be eligible the project must:[77]

i. Be green according to ACGF green framework.

ii. Be bankable. Projects that exhibit one of the following may meet the bankable requirements: negative rate of return, rate of return less than normal market thresholds in the project location, or rate of return above normal market thresholds but less than what would be required for a green infrastructure project (risk-adjusted considering associated additional costs).

iii. Catalyse private capital flow. For example, the project must have a roadmap for private capital flow that accounts for at least 20%, structuring support by the facility, and have a sovereign guarantee for ACGF Funds.[78]

A more detailed description of eligibility criteria can be accessed at ACGF's Principles and Eligibility Criteria

The Green Recovery Platform that was launched at COP26 aims to develop and finance green infrastructure projects that align with the ambitions of the Paris Agreement. The platform aspires to use USD665m of development funds, and catalyse an additional USD7bn for green infrastructure across ASEAN.[79]

"Within the ACGF we are following a phased approach to supporting de-risking in green projects. The initial phase of support, which is being undertaken now, is using the classic approach of providing concessional finance for reducing the blended cost of capital for a project for an initial 7 years which covers construction and initial operations. At the end of this period, the ACGF funding cost steps up, with the intention of focusing projects to consider refinancing ACGF out using commercial finance – we thus achieve the aim of leveraging at the start of a project, as well as catalyzing private investments once the risks are considerably reduced. ADB, as administrator of the AIF, is also exploring providing other innovative de-risking measures in future phases of the AIF. An example of this is support for operations in the first 3–5 years through a minimum revenue guarantee support. Whilst still using a debt instrument for this, this provides further necessary de-risking to projects especially needed if suffering from the impacts of the COVID-19 pandemic. We are also exploring adding a first loss product to provide guarantees to projects which are trying to raise commercial finance or even through bonds. The rollout of these products will of course depend on projects, governments, and our own AIF Board considerations."

Anouj Mehta, country director Thailand Resident Mission and unit head of the ACGF, ADB.

Source: ASEAN Catalytic Green Finance Facility Overivew

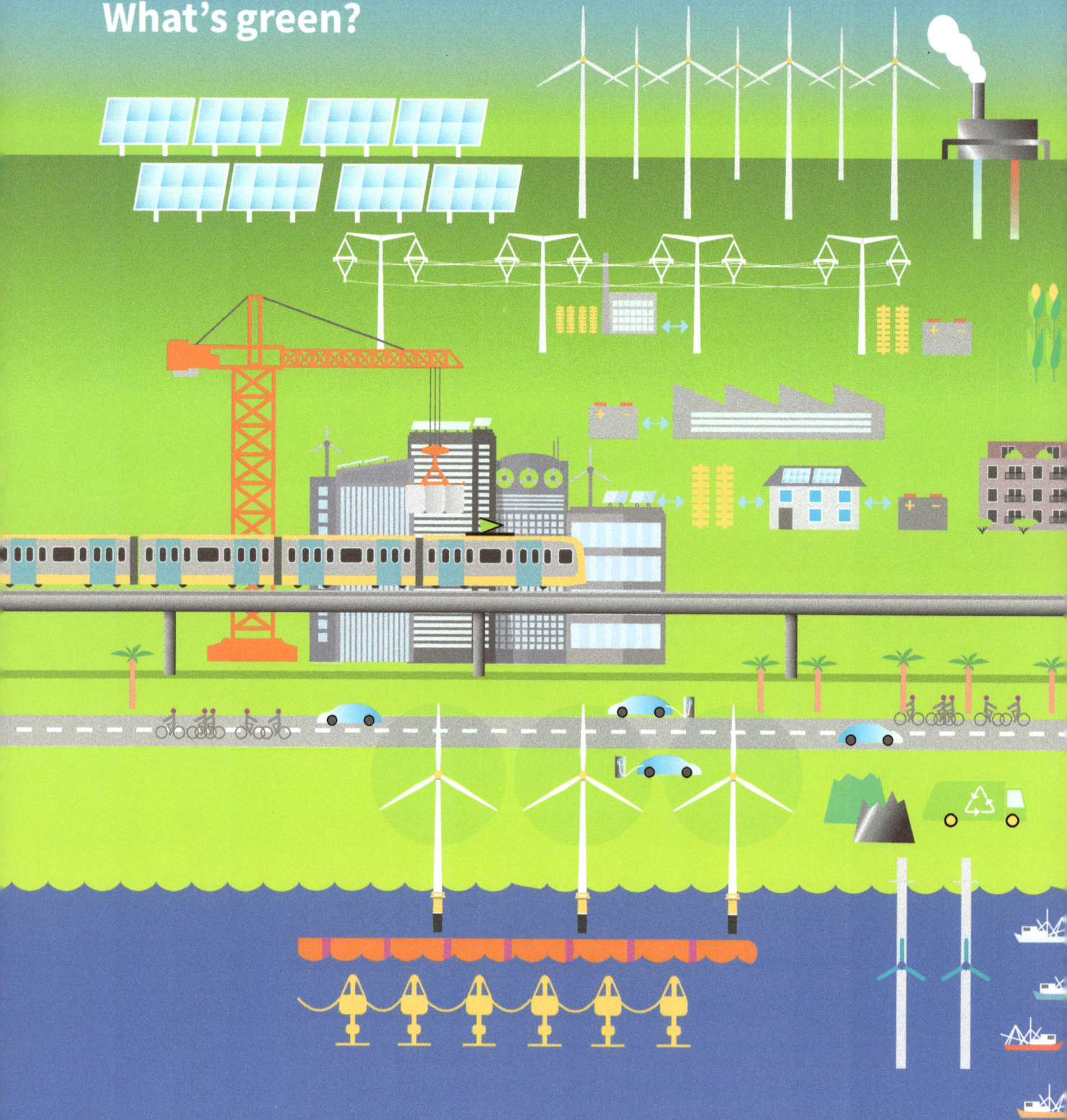

What's green?

Geothermal:

According to the Geothermal Energy Association, 39 countries could supply 100% of their electricity needs from geothermal energy, yet only 6% to 7% of the world's potential geothermal power has been tapped.[80]

Drawdown Agenda

Solar:

The world installed a record number of new solar power projects in 2017, more than net additions of coal, gas and nuclear plants put together.[82]

UNFCCC

Hydropower:

Hydropower is the largest source of renewable electricity in the world, producing around 17% of the world's electricity from over 1 200 GW of installed capacity, and is expected to remain the world's largest source of renewable electricity generation by 2022.[81]

International Energy Agency

Transport (rail):

75% of the world's countries have established strategies and targets to improve the environmental performance of their transport sector within their Intended Nationally Determined Contributions (INDCs). One-fifth of the transport-related (I)NDCs include measures in the railway sector.[83]

UNFCCC

Water:

The UN says the planet is facing a 40% shortfall in water supply by 2030, unless the world dramatically improves the management of this precious resource.[84]

UNFCCC

Buildings:

Building-related emissions account for about one-third of global GHG emissions and could double by 2050, making building efficiency a critical part of the COP21 agenda.[85]

GreenBiz

© Climate Bonds Initiative

3. Green infrastructure investment opportunities

Renewable energy

Energy generation, transmission or storage technology that has low or zero carbon emissions. This can include solar energy, wind energy, bioenergy, hydropower, geothermal energy, marine energy or any other renewable energy source.

Investing in renewable energy can bolster the green recovery of Indonesia

The pandemic has created an economic shock nationwide including in the energy sector. To mitigate this impact, the government has channelled at least USD6.78bn towards energy.[86] This spending includes the expansion of electricity subsidies to protect 31m of the poorest households of Indonesia; a critical safety net.[87]

The majority of this budget was earmarked to subsidise fossil fuel energy. At least USD6.54bn was spent on fossil fuel in the last stimulus programme, while spending on renewables only amounted to USD240m.[88] Overall, green energy only accounted for 3.5% of the total stimulus spending from the national economic recovery programme, indicating that the previous rounds of stimulus have not prioritised clean and green energy.[89]

Energy will be key in driving the economic recovery of Indonesia. Prioritising green energy in Indonesia would boost green recovery while making progress in decarbonisation. Renewable energy spending should be increased in future stimulus packages. Decarbonising energy is also critical to achieving climate ambitions of Indonesia, as energy is the second largest national source of emissions at 39%, only after forest and land use.[90] Transitioning away from fossil fuels will also minimise the risk of locking future emissions and exposure to stranded assets, especially for coal plants.[91]

Sector overview

Fossil fuels—especially thermal coal plants—still dominate the Indonesian energy mix (74.4% of the energy mix as of 2020).[92] The government has recently rolled out a plan to phase out coal plants.[93] This includes retiring coal plants earlier to achieve net-zero by 2060 or sooner. Some analyses have cited that this target could be achieved much sooner with sufficient regulatory framework and investments.[94] The recent call from the government for a coal moratorium in 2025 is an optimistic development.

Figure 2: Renewable Installed Capacity by type in Indonesia, September 2021

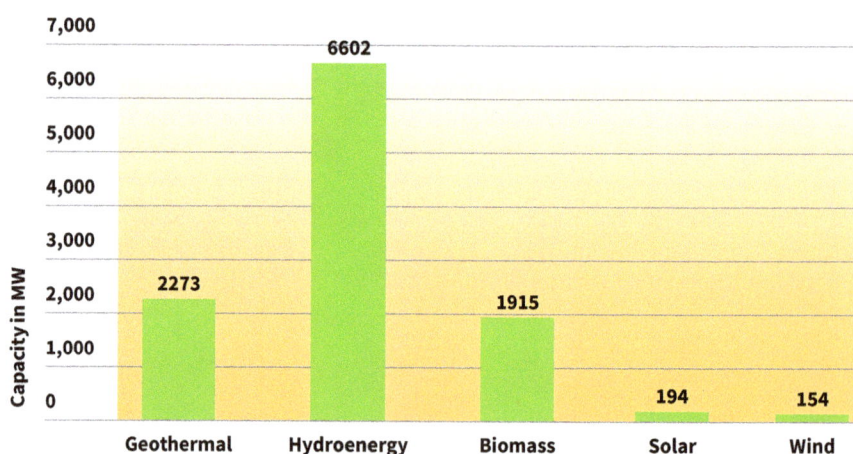

Source: Ministry of Energy and Mineral Resources 2022 [104]

Indonesia has set a target to achieve 23% renewable in the energy mix by 2025, and recently sent a strong signal for renewable energy growth moving forward. The latest electrification development plan of Indonesia (RUPTL) 2021–2030 published in October 2021 has increased the renewable energy target to 51.6% of the energy mix by 2030, compared to only 30% from the prior plan.[95] This is also the first time the renewable energy target has been larger than the fossil fuel share, which is 48.4% by 2030.[96]

The abundant natural sources of renewable energy in Indonesia are still heavily under-utilised. In 2020, total installed renewable energy capacity only reached 10 gigawatts out of 417 gigawatts renewable resources available (i.e., 2.5% of available resources).[97] Hydropower and geothermal are the largest contributors while solar energy remains under-utilised.

As of June 2021, renewable energy accounted for an 11.4% share of the national energy mix and, to achieve the 2025 target, Indonesia needs to double this and deliver an additional 14 gigawatt capacity.[98] This would require a massive investment of USD154bn by 2025.[99]

The investment poured into renewable projects—complemented by a favourable policy ecosystem—will determine how rapidly Indonesia can deploy its renewable energy plants. However, the restrictive and relatively opaque procurement rules and uncertainty in contract negotiations and power purchase agreements (PPAs) are still hampering the growth of renewable energy projects in Indonesia.[100] These barriers cause uncertainty for independent power producers and limit the bankability of renewable projects.

Further policy reform that improves the bankability of renewable energy projects could attract more green capital. As of 2021, the PPA and tariff scheme has not resulted in predictable cash flow, limiting investor confidence.[101] The upcoming presidential regulation on renewable energy tariffs—a regulation highly anticipated by market players—is intended to address this. This is a positive step towards boosting renewables investment.

More profitable pricing schemes for renewable projects could improve project bankability and boost the confidence of private investors.

Favourable regulations—especially for solar rooftops—are already in place. To support the 6,500 megawatts (MW) of installed solar power capacity target by 2025, the Ministry of Energy and Mineral Resources introduced regulation No. 26 of 2021. This regulation eliminates the discounted price for solar energy exported to PLN, the sole power buyer of the country. Before this new regulation, solar energy exporters could only sell the electricity at a discounted price. This financial incentive is expected to spur the growth of domestic solar PV installations and industry, and potentially promote green jobs. In 2018, the government also required that all government building rooftops have at least 30% of solar panel coverage. This regulation facilitated the growth of solar roofs from 592 consumers in 2018, to 3,781 consumers in 2021.[102]

In 2020, the government also removed the build, own, operate, and transfer requirement for—and improved the commercial viability of—renewable projects. Many developers said that the old scheme undermined project bankability.[103]

Type		Incentives
Tax incentive	Tax and duty allowances	An investment tax deduction equivalent to 30% of fixed capital investment, applied as 5% over 6 years for renewable energy developers and investors, among other benefits.[105]
Tax incentive	Tax holiday	Provision of Corporate Income Tax Reduction Facilities provides corporate income tax holidays for investment in pioneer industries including renewable energy power plants as stated in Badan Koordinasi Penanaman Modal (Investment Coordinating Board) Regulation 1/2019 as amended by 6/2019.[106]
De-risking	Geothermal Resource Risk Mitigation Facility (GREM)	Provides financing and risk mitigation facilities for geothermal exploration activities. The risk sharing mechanism is particularly important during high risk geothermal exploration because if an exploration failure occurred the developer would not fully bear the risks and costs of exploration. GREM is financed by multilateral development banks and multilateral donors.[107]
Financial incentive	Regulation No. 26 of 2021 on Solar PV	This regulation incentivises solar PV owners by providing a better net-metering tariff, a longer reset period, expansion to a non-PLN business area, and overall a more efficient application process.
		Owners of PV systems can receive credit for the surplus electricity they provide to the grid with a multiplier of 100%. This is larger than the previous multiplier of 65%.[108]

Table 4: Fiscal and non-fiscal incentives and de-risking mechanisms for Renewable Energy developers, 2021.

Source: Ministry of Energy and Mineral Resources (MEMR)

Investment pathways

Indonesia requires USD154bn of investments to achieve the renewable target of 23% by 2025, and public funding is expected to only cover 51% of this requirement.[109] The pandemic may cause further setbacks, as portions of the public budget have been diverted. In this context, the role of the private sector becomes increasingly critical for Indonesia to achieve its 2025 target and enable a sustainable recovery.[110]

Non-state financing plays an important role in renewable investments. According to past renewable financing trends, private finance, DFIs, and credit export agencies financed 58% of renewables during 2016–2019.[111]

Most renewable energy projects are eligible to be financed using green bonds. Conversely, most of the green bonds issued by Indonesian entities up until 2021 have included renewable energy as a component of the Use-of-Proceeds (UoP).

Green bonds can be structured in several ways, including project bonds, corporate bonds, covered bonds, or Asset Backed Securities (ABS). Aggregation of smaller projects can be done through securitisation or by banks originating green loans and refinancing in the green bond market. This structuring is particularly beneficial for smaller scale renewable projects in Indonesia.

State-owned banks—such as Mandiri Bank, Bank Rakyat Indonesia, and Bank Negara Indonesia—are providing soft loans for residential households that would like to install solar rooftops.[112] This financial incentive is intended to spur the uptake of domestic solar.

Municipal governments are also potential issuers of green bonds. So far, complex regulatory challenges and bureaucratic requirements have prevented municipal governments from entering the market.[113] Adjusting regulatory requirements—such as lowering the debt service coverage ratio or streamlining the approval process—would encourage municipal green bond issuance.[114]

SOEs should consider issuing green bonds to finance their projects, as clean energy projects are easily suitable for inclusion in green bonds. Indonesia has seen positive development towards green bond by the two major energy SOEs: Indonesia State Electricity Utility Company (PLN), and Indonesia State-Owned Oil Company (PERTAMINA). Both SOEs have announced that they will issue a green bond in 2022.[115] In October 2021, PLN—in partnership with ADB—launched the Statement of Intent for Sustainable Financing. This document looks at project eligibility, framework development, and external review, and will help in both pre- and post-issuances of this green bond programme. This deal could pave the way for other SOEs to issue sustainability bonds.

Construction of the 943 MW Matenggeng Hydroelectric Power Plant

Proponent: State Electricity Company (PLN)

Location: West Java

Status: Planned (Operational by 2025)

Classification: Hydropower, generation facilities and infrastructure

Description: The upper dam of this plant will be built in the Cimancing river, lower dam on the Citeuteul river, and one of the tributaries at the Citanduy river. The construction of this plant will involve a 500 kV transmission line consisting of 2 lines, each with a length of 28.4 kmr and 28.3 kmr and power station substation 500 kV[116]

Output: This plant will supply 943MW of renewable energy peaking power to the Java-Bali grid.

Cost: USD1.04bn (looking for a USD826.9m of additional loan)

Financial structure: State-Owned Enterprise, Loan

Blawan Ijen 110 MW Geothermal Project

Title: Ijen Geothermal Plant (2x55MW)

Proponent: PT Medco Cahaya Geothermal

Location: Banyuwangi and Situbondo Regency, East Java Province

Status: Planned (exploration phase)

Classification: Generating facilities, geothermal, energy

Description: This project will have a capacity of 2 x 55 Megawatt (MW) power generation and approximately 28 km transmission line to the nearest substation (Banyuwangi Substation).[117]

Output: This plant will provide a source of renewable electricity supply to the Java grid. This project will reduce Java dependency on coal plants, as coal dominates the source of electricity in Java at the moment.

Cost: Approx. USD165m[118]

Financial structure: Joint Venture PT Medco Power Indonesia and Ormat International Inc.

Low-Carbon Transport

Transportation modes and ancillary infrastructure that produce low or zero direct carbon emissions. This can include national and urban passenger rail and freight rail networks, Bus Rapid Transit (BRT) systems, electric vehicles, and bicycle transport systems.

Railway infrastructure is one of the key investment areas for climate change mitigation.[119] The Indonesian railway and rolling stock infrastructure construction will require around USD65bn of investments during 2021–2030, and state-budget will only cover around 36%.[120] Most railway infrastructure qualifies as green, hence is suitable for inclusion in a green bond. State-owned entities taking a blended finance approach could consider raising funds through green bonds. Rolling out green transportation infrastructure offers employment opportunities that could form part of the post COVID-19 economic recovery. IFC estimates that by 2030, green transportation across EM will create 53.4 million direct jobs.[121]

Sector Overview

Transport in Indonesia in 2016 contributed around 26% of total national greenhouse gas (GHG) emissions.[122] Without decarbonisation, emissions will continue to rise in the future as the sector consumption is expected to grow by 5.2% annually until 2040.[123]

In 2020, approximately 93% of land vehicles were powered by petroleum based fuel, while only 7% were powered by biofuel.[124] Since transport makes up 27% of energy-related GHG emissions, decarbonising the national energy mix cannot be successful without also electrifying the transport system.

The high rate of motorisation in large cities is causing urban problems such as traffic congestion and air pollution. According to an analysis by ADB, emissions from transport on average contribute 70% to 80% of outdoor air pollution in large urban areas.[125] The Jakarta Post and BAPPENAS estimated that the heavy congestion in Jakarta is causing an annual loss of USD5bn (IDR65tn).[126] Decarbonising transport is not only important for curbing national GHG emissions, but also critical to improving the overall urban health and air quality, especially in big cities like Jakarta and Surabaya.

Connectivity remains a priority nationally, and with enough investments and focus on mass transport and clean vehicles, the future of transportation in Indonesia can be sustainable. The long term climate strategy document of the country envisions a greener transportation system by limiting fossil fuel based vehicles and expanding railways and urban transport networks.[127] The growth of motorisation is concentrated in larger cities like Jakarta and Bandung. As a result, large cities are experiencing increasing congestion and air pollution problems.

Through Government Regulation No. 33 of 2021 for the railway sector, the government has streamlined the regulatory process to further improve the ease of doing business in the railway sector.[128] This new regulation repealed and replaced several regulatory related articles from the older regulation in 2017.

The future of green transport in Indonesia will include the expansion of the rail network, the addition of high-speed rail routes and upgrades to the rolling stock from diesel to electric, and the expansion of zero emission vehicles. There will also be an expansion and upgrade of the bus rapid transit systems, more interconnectivity with other modes of public transport, and more hybrid buses.

Half of the government National Strategic Projects pipeline are dedicated to transport infrastructure, with just under a quarter of these being green infrastructure. There is scope for even further investment, particularly for rail and bus rapid transit development as well as zero emission vehicles and sustainable waterborne transport in the future.

Investment pathways

Many funding structures are available to encourage private sector involvement in the long-term financing required for low-carbon transport projects including green bonds, outright asset acquisitions, public–private partnerships (PPPs) and the securitisation of green assets.

The government has offered multiple railway projects for private investors or a PPP scheme, and prioritises a blended finance scheme for railway funding. A notable example of this is the Makassar-Parepare railway project. The project secured a senior term syndicated loan ofIDR693.83bn (USD48m) with PT Indonesia Infrastructure Finance and PT SMI, and a sharia financing agreement with PT Bank Syariah Indonesia Tbk.[129] The construction of this project will be partially funded from the proceeds of a sovereign sukuk.[130]

A sovereign sukuk—or a bond—is a common instrument for railway financing in Indonesia. During 2018–2019, the government raised at leastIDR1.7tn from issuing sovereign sukuks to finance railway infrastructure.[131] Railway assets almost always qualify as green expenditures, making them ideal Use-of-Proceeds for green bonds, sovereign or otherwise.

Several SOEs responsible for rail have already issued bonds for transport works. For example, in 2017, state-owned railway operator PT Kereta Api Indonesia listed bonds worth IDR2tn (USD148m) on the Jakarta Stock Exchange.[132]

Future bonds from these SOEs and corporations should be issued as green bonds to raise their profile as sustainable investments. As private sector appetite increases, funding sources will continue to diversify and investment will accelerate. Investors seeking exposure to low-carbon transport projects and assets should consider the various investment pathways available. For instance, government-owned low-carbon transport assets are often identified in their green bond offerings. This pathway provides indirect exposure for investors to specific projects and assets and provides attractive credit and liquidity credentials for institutional investors.

More direct investment pathways include participation in consortium debt arrangements and/or equity stakes in individual projects via PPPs or other public–private ownership and financing structures.

Jakarta MRT Phase 4 Project, Fatmawati – Taman Mini Indonesia Indah (TMII) Route

Proponent: PT MRT Jakarta

Location: South Jakarta

Status: Planned (looking for private investors)

Classification: Trains, public passenger transport, transport

Description: MRT Phase 4 construction is targeted to begin in 2022 with an expected completion date of 2027. This railway will be approximately 12km long. This route will consist of seven underground stations, three elevated stations, and one depot. This route will be integrated with other modes of public transport such as MRT Lebak Bulus-Bundaran Hotel Indonesia, Jabodetabek LRT, commuter line, and Transjakarta Bus.[133]

Output: At the moment, this route does not consist of any railway based transport.[134] When this line is built, it will be the only railway-based transportation connecting the two points. Due to the high density of this area, this corridor is expected to carry 124,000 passengers per day.

Cost: IDR28tn (USD1.96bn)

Financial structure: Government bonds, public-private partnerships (PPPs), EPC contract, G2G financing[135]

LRT Kelapa Gading – Jakarta International Stadium (JIS) Route[136]

Proponent: PT Jakarta Propertindo

Location: North Jakarta

Status: Planned (market sounding)

Classification: Trains, public passenger transport, transport

Description: This rail route will be 8km long and will be connected to an existing LRT network. The total line will consist of six stations, and construction will take around two years to complete.

Output: By 2025, this train is expected to carry 71,358 passengers. The construction of this line contributes to easing traffic congestion in Jakarta.

Cost: IDR6.6tn (USD462m)

Financial structure: PPP, EPC

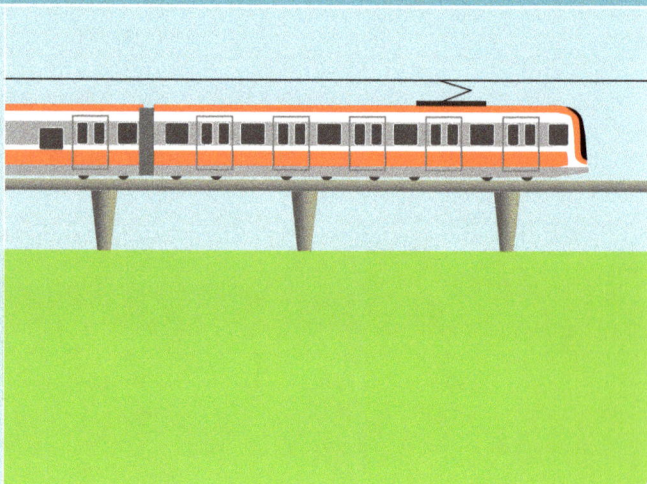

Sustainable Water

Assets that do not increase greenhouse gas emissions or that aim at emission reductions over the operational lifetime of the asset, address adaptation, and increase the resilience of surrounding environments. These assets cover built as well as nature-based water infrastructure.

Water management projects could include water capture and collection, water storage, water treatment (with methane emissions treatment), flood defence, drought defence, stormwater management, and ecological restoration and management.

Sector overview

Dense urban and coastal areas in Indonesia are vulnerable to flood hazards. During 2000–2020, floods impacted the population of Indonesia more than any other natural and climate disaster.[137] The intensity of flooding in Indonesia is becoming more frequent: from 679 flood incidents in 2018 to 1,062 in 2021.[138] Flood disasters are largely influenced by rising sea levels, poor urban planning, land-use changes, and deforestation.[139]

Flood resilience and mitigation infrastructure is a priority for the government. The National Medium Term Plan has set several flood control and dam projects as a priority during 2020–2024.[140] The government has built abundant flood control and protection infrastructure and is planning to build even more.[141] During 2015–2019, the government constructed 1,305 km of flood mitigation infrastructure, and a coastal protection zone spanning 179 km.[142]

Clean water supply—especially for drinking and irrigation—is still a challenge for many remote areas of Indonesia.[143] In 2020, the populations of Bengkulu and Papua Provinces had the lowest access to clean water, both with only 62% coverage.[144] Nationally, safe drinking water coverage is at 72%.[145] The government plans to scale up water supply infrastructure and set a target of 100% access to safe drinking water by 2024.[146] The private sector will have to provide 27% of the investments. [147]

In urban settings like Jakarta, many of the challenges around water provision and availability are related to water use and management. Subsidence is due to the extraction of groundwater for drinking and bathing; as water is pumped out, the land above it sinks. Groundwater is pumped so extensively because rivers are too polluted to be a healthy water source in most cities. Large engineering solutions have been being proposed to deal with subsidence (such as a USD40bn giant sea wall in Jakarta).

Both water provision and flood control infrastructure are priorities for the Government of Indonesia and municipal authorities, as demonstrated in the National Medium Term Plan 2020–2024. Planning for future cities needs to integrate climate disaster risk planning, especially flooding as urban infrastructure is exposed to high risks from flood hazards.

Enhanced planning processes and increased upfront investment will be required for water infrastructure to meet the challenges of climate change and rapid urbanisation.

Investment pathways

The government requires IDR253.8tn to achieve the 2024 safe drinking water goal.[148] State and regional government budgets can only cover around 74% of this funding need, leaving 27% to be financed by the private sector under the PPP scheme.[149]

The majority of water infrastructure in Indonesia is publicly owned and managed by state- and local-owned enterprises. Although this is unlikely to change in the medium-term, PPP can enable private participation.

Attracting private investors would require innovative approaches to financing. Instruments such as green bonds should be considered as an investment pathway. Provincial governments could raise money by issuing municipal bonds.[150] Proceeds from such bonds could be distributed to local water providers (Perusahaan Daerah Air Minum) to finance water infrastructure projects.

In ASEAN, water utilities such as Manila Water Corporation have issued sustainability bonds. Manila Water issued a 5-year USD500m sustainability bond with proceeds allocated towards refinancing debt and funding infrastructure capital expenditure in the company concession area in Metro Manila.[151]

Multipurpose Merangin Dam Infrastructure Project

Proponent: Directorate General for Water Resources, Ministry of Public Works and Housing

Location: Jambi, Central Sumatra and West Sumatra

Status: Planned

Classification: Water infrastructure, flood defences and water distribution and hydropower, generation facilities and infrastructure

Description: This dam is aligned with Indonesia's RPJMN 2020 – 2024. This dam has a multifunctional purpose of providing irrigation, flood control, clean water supply and possibly providing electricity supply. The dimension for this dam is 335m x 14 m x 94m

Output: This dam will provide 25.75-meter cube/second of irrigation for 12.000 ha for food production. This dam will have the capacity of 200-meter cube per second for flood control and provide a clean water supply of 500 litres per second.

Cost: Estimated IDR 2.64tn to 4.77tn (Approx. USD334m)

Financial structure: PPP, Design-Build-Finance-Maintain-Transfer (DBFOMT)

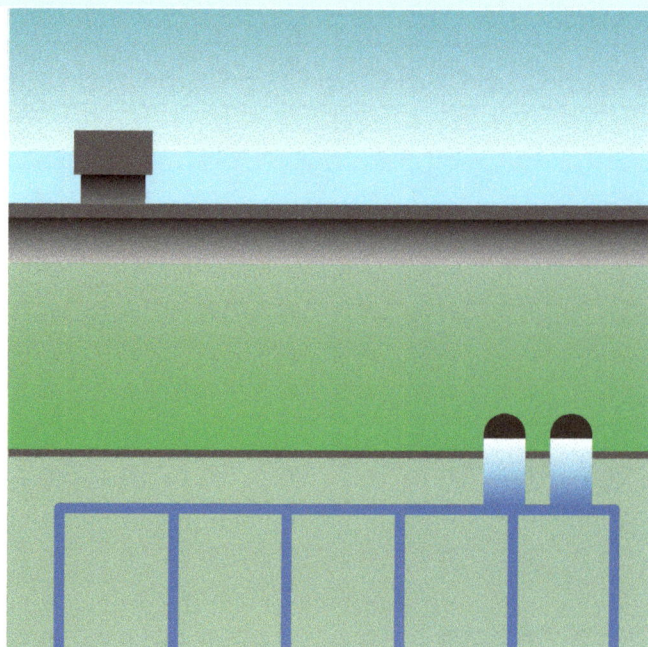

North Java Coasts Management and Coastal Protection Project

Proponent: Directorate General of Water Resources, Ministry of Public Works and Housing

Location: Coasts of North Java

Status: Planned

Classification: Water treatment, water infrastructure, water

Description: This project will involve the construction of 24.05km flow normalisation, 12.05 flood control channels, 10km of embankment, 4 sets of water sluice, 1 set of water pump, 2 sets of flood canal and a 11.8 km seawall.

Output: This project will improve the climate adaptation and resilience capacity for Java coastal areas. This project protect 28.000 ha of flooded area, 67.775 ha of residential area, and 16.4 km of coastline.

Cost: USD605m (USD500m covered by ADB loan, USD5m by state budget. Requires another USD50m loan[152])

Financial structure: Loan

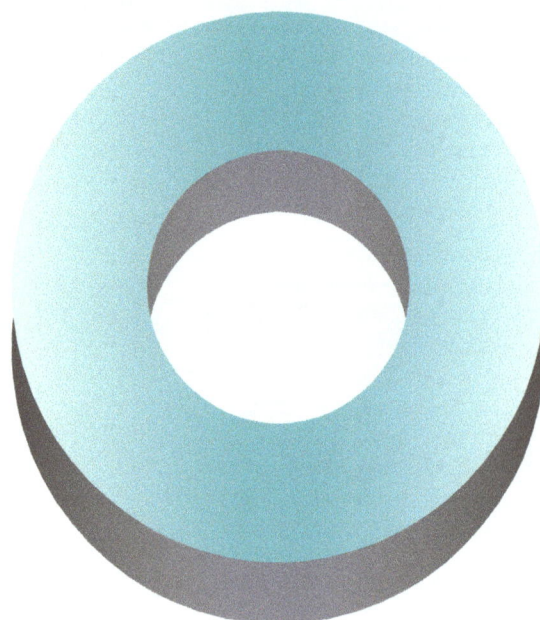

♻ Sustainable Waste

The efficient use of resources to cut down on waste production, coupled with collection and disposal systems that promote reuse and recycle, thereby minimising residual waste going into energy from waste facilities. Where waste must go to landfill, there are gas capture systems installed to minimise emissions as well as measures to minimise run-off and other negative impacts on surrounding environ ments.

Sector overview

Scaling up waste management infrastructure is critical for Indonesia as it is experiencing a waste emergency. Indonesia is the second-largest producer of plastic waste in the world. Plastic marine debris pollution is the result of uncollected waste and plastic leakage. Even though the government has been battling this, in 2020 Indonesia collected only around 59.7% of its solid waste.[153] The collected waste mostly goes to landfill.

With half of the population of the country living in urban areas, almost 40% of urban residents still do not have access to waste collection.[154] Waste collection coverage in rural areas is even lower, and as a result 85% of plastic waste in rural areas remains uncollected.[155] Of total plastic waste, only around 10% is recycled.[156]

Uncollected waste is a major issue in Indonesia. This is mainly because open dumping and burning are common outcomes for uncollected waste. Approximately 81% of urban solid waste in Indonesia is not recycled and ends up going to landfill, causing leakages into rivers and oceans.[157]

In response, the government committed to developing a comprehensive strategy to improve policy and institutional capacity for localised waste management; enhance the management capacity of urban waste water; reduce landfill waste by promoting the Reduce, Reuse, Recycle slogan; and turn waste into energy.

Waste-to-energy has become central to the government waste management strategy, with 15 waste-to-energy plants planned for development in 12 cities during 2021–2030.[158] These plants will be able to produce 234 MW of electricity, and process around 16,000 tonnes of solid waste per day.[159] Many corporations are starting to build plastic recycling facilities in 2021.

As long as these facilities undertake adequate sorting and removal of plastics and metals, they will make a substantial contribution to the achievement of both national waste reduction and low-emission energy targets.

The government launched the National Partnership Action Plan in 2020, which is a master plan to reduce plastic and solid waste. In the plan, the government has set a goal of reducing marine plastic debris by 70% and solid waste by 30%, and to handle 70% of solid waste by 2025. The Ministries of Maritime Affairs, and Environment and Forestry will work with the private sector and civil society groups—as well as global partners—to identify solutions for plastic pollution and develop a corresponding investment strategy. This initiative is part of the Global Plastic Action Partnership, which uses an innovative, analytical model for data-driven decision making that estimates the investment needed, timeline, environmental footprint and greenhouse gas emissions, as well as the impact of projects on the lives of people.

Investment pathways

Approximately USD18.4bn is required by 2040 to build adequate waste management infrastructure in Indonesia.[160] Around USD8bn should be allocated to plastic waste.[161] Provincial and city governments are ultimately responsible for waste management implementation, but they remain underfunded. Relying on local budgets alone is not sufficient.

Most of the major waste management assets and projects in Indonesia are publicly owned, with public financing used primarily for waste treatment facilities, waste-to-energy processing, and sanitary refill infrastructure. Waste treatment facilities usually demand significant capital. An investment pathway for sustainable waste infrastructure could be through green bonds issued by local governments.

There are also new facilities proposed for development via PPPs. In this case, investment pathways include participation in consortium debt deals and/or equity stakes in individual projects via PPPs or other public–private ownership and financing structures.

Privately owned assets and projects—which include recycling facilities and some waste-to-energy facilities—offer other means of debt and equity investment. Many fast-moving consumer goods corporations which are major plastic producing entities are constructing recycling facilities.

Waste-to-Energy Refused Derived Fuel Plant in Bantar Gebang[162]

Proponent: Government of Jakarta

Location: Jakarta

Status: Planned (market sounding)

Classification: Waste to energy plants (e.g. incineration, gasification, pyrolysis and plasma), waste to energy, waste and pollution control

Description: Bantar Gebang, one of the world's largest landfill sites, is predicted to reach overcapacity in 2022. This RFD plant is intended to address this. Source of revenue of this project will come from tipping fee and sales of the plant itself.

Output: This facility will be able to produce 750 tons of RDF for every 1000 tons of solid waste.[163]

Cost: IDR1.5tn (USD105m)

Financial structure: Public Private Partnership (PPP)

Jatibarang Waste-to-Energy Plant in Semarang

Proponent: Regent of Semarang

Location: Semarang, Central Java

Status: Planned (pre-feasibility study stage, COD 2023)

Classification: Waste to energy plants (e.g. incineration, gasification, pyrolysis and plasma), waste to energy, waste and pollution control

Description: This facility will process the municipal waste from 18 districts in Semarang and will employ a moving grate incinerator waste-to-energy technology. This plant will have a feed in tariff of USD13.35 cent/kWh.

Output: This facility will have the capacity to process 1000 tons of municipal solid waste per day and supply 19.3 MW of electricity

Cost: IDR 3.2tn (USD224m)

Financial structure: PPP, Build-Operate-Transfer (BOT)

4. Recommendations

The growth of green infrastructure pipelines and associated green finance (including the green bond market) in Indonesia could be accelerated by key policy and institutional changes. Such measures could aim to prioritise green infrastructure for future stimulus spending, raise the profile of green infrastructure, support critical finance channels for infrastructure development stakeholders, and create more options for investors. Six suggested measures are:

Incorporate climate risk exposure and ESG criteria into new infrastructure plans, including during PPP preparation. Account for future depreciation of assets due to change in precipitation patterns, temperature increases, and extreme weather events. Fossil fuel assets are categorised high climate risk assets.

Introduce financial incentives for green, social, and sustainability (GSS) bond issuers. This could take the form of exempting the pre- or post-issuance cost for issuing a green bond, such as waiving the verification and external reviewer fee, or reducing or exempting of the listing fee altogether.

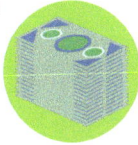

Promote "COVID-19 Recovery" bond programmes and exclude assets that are at risk from future shocks or at risk of being stranded— like fossil fuels assets—to support a green recovery. The issuance of green, resilience and/or blue bonds can support a more sustainable recovery. The USD750m sovereign green tranches from 2020 and 2021 are examples of COVID-19 recovery bonds and can be replicated in the future. Asset selection should exclude activities that are at risk from future shocks or assets that can become stranded because of climate policy changes, or which are not resilient to physical climate risks.

Promote blended finance and de-risking, credit enhancement, or guarantee mechanisms for green transactions to improve the bankability of an infrastructure project. Global multilateral development banks could help to catalyse the local green bond market by providing credit enhancement in the form of guarantees or the taking of first loss.

Encourage state-owned enterprises (SOEs) to issue green bonds to finance ongoing green infrastructure projects to complement state-budget financing. The Makassar – Parepare railway—which is funded partially by a sukuk—is an example of this. In the future, SOEs could consider a similar financing scheme where sukuks or bonds are issued as green.

Promote municipal green bonds. This could include incentives such as credit enhancement for local governments or establishing green municipal finance for local governments to aggregate debt requirements and access lower costs of capital. The government could also consider lowering the debt service coverage ratio criteria for short- or medium-term bonds to allow flexibility for municipal governments.

Annex I: Green financial instruments, Indonesia

Equity structure	Debt Instrument	Indonesian example
Islamic finance, including Sukuk	Supranational and sovereign green bonds	The Republic of Indonesia issued a USD1.25bn 5-year green sovereign sukuk in 2018 to finance eligible projects under a range of categories: Renewable Energy, Energy Efficiency, Adaptation, Transport, Green Buildings, Sustainable Agriculture, Sustainable Management of Natural Resources, and Green Tourism.[164]
Public–private partnership	Sub-sovereign green bonds	State-owned infrastructure financing company PT Sarana Multi Infrastruktur (Indonesia) issued a 2-tranche IDR500bn (USD50m) unsecured green bond in 2018. Proceeds were allocated to refinancing three light rail transit projects, two mini hydropower plants, a water treatment plant and irrigation systems.[165]
		PT SMI supports the government infrastructure development agenda for Indonesia through partnerships with private and/or multilateral financial institutions in PPP projects.[166] It facilitates infrastructure financing, project development, and infrastructure advisory services.
Joint venture, public–private partnership	Green bond, sustainability bond	The Tropical Landscape Finance Facility—a partnership between the United Nations Environment Programme, World Agroforestry Centre, ADM Capital and BNP Paribas—launched its landmark USD95m bonds to help finance a sustainable natural rubber plantation on heavily degraded land in two provinces in Indonesia.[167]
	Green loan	The World Bank is providing a loan of USD150m to support the Indonesia Geothermal Resource Risk Mitigation (GREM) project. The loan from the World Bank will support public and private developers to lower risks in geothermal resources exploration.[168]
Infrastructure/property funds		Indonesian Infrastructure Finance is a state-owned company that provides infrastructure financing and advisory services for viable infrastructure projects. In December 2018, it provided USD28.7m financing for the project company to develop a 2×5 MW Mini Hydro Power Plant Project in North Sumatra. The project is to fulfil the electricity demand for the North Sumatra region where the electricity demand is projected to grow by 10% annually until 2027. During 2011–2017, the increase in demand ranged from 5% to 8%.[169]
Viability Gap Funding		Viability Gap Funding is a form of financial support provided by the Indonesian Ministry of Finance to improve the certainty and viability of PPP infrastructure projects. The Bandar Lampung Water Supply project is a joint project between the government and the private sector to increase the coverage of drinking water services for citizens in Bandar Lampung from 20% (2015) to 46% (2024) and improve environmental sanitation, living standards, and public health. Other PPP project examples include Umbulan and West Semarang Water Project.[170]

Annex II: Sample Green Pipeline

Methodology

The sample pipeline consists of a list of green and potentially green projects in the seven sectors: low carbon and/or sustainable transport, renewable energy, sustainable water management, and sustainable waste management. The greenness selection criteria are based on the Climate Bonds Taxonomy (in the back cover).

An analysis of key government project pipelines and various projects owned by different proponents show that there are various green projects of different sizes and technologies spread across the country. These pipelines are obtained mainly from the official infrastructure project list by the **National Strategic Projects list in the Committee for Acceleration**

of Priority Infrastructure Delivery (KPPIP) pipeline, the National Medium Term Development Plan 2020 – 2024 (RPJMN 2020 – 2024), the Minister of National Economic Development and Planning (BAPPENAS)'s List of Medium-Term Planned External Loans, widely known as the Blue Book 2020-2024, derived from Indonesia's RPJMN, PPP Book 2021, the PT Sarana Multi Infrastruktur pipeline. This analysis also includes projects from the Asian Development Bank (ADB), various media sources such as articles, press releases, and other ministerial departments.

Project Status

These metrics were used to classify the green infrastructure investment opportunities by status

Completed: High profile, recently completed projects, including projects that are currently operational

Under construction: Major projects from national, state, and local government pipelines that are under construction

Planned/Planning: Major projects from national, state, and local government pipelines that have not yet begun construction but have been announced and undergone business case planning and/or have an allocated budget. Planned project are projects that have been approved by the government bodies. Projects at planning stages are projects that are either waiting for relevant government bodies at pre-construction stage, at procurement stage, undergoing fesibility studies, or under development.

Green Project							
Setor	Project name	Location	Cost (USD)	Status	Greenness	Pipeline source	Notes
Low carbon transport	LRT Gading-Jakarta International Stadium (JIS)	Jakarta	USD462 (IDR6.6tn)[171]	Planned	Green	Jakarta City Government	Market sounding[172]
	MRT Phase 3 Kalideres-Ujung Menteng (East – West Line)	Jakarta	USD3.8bn (IDR55tn)	Planned	Green	RPJMN 2020 – 2024	Seeking USD106m loan[173]
	MRT Phase 4 Fatmawati-TMII	South Jakarta	USD1.96bn (IDR28tn)[174]	Planned	Green	Jakarta City Government	Seeking for private investors
	MRT Jakarta (North – South Corridor)	Jakarta	USD2.76bn (IDR39.5tn)	Completed	Green	Jakarta City Government	
	Transit Oriented Development (TOD) Pegangsaan Dua	Jakarta	USD103m (IDR1.5tn)	Planned	Green	Jakarta City Government	Market sounding
	Jakarta – Surabaya Railway	Jakarta – East Java	USD7.2bn (IDR102.37tn)[175]	Under construction	Green	National Strategic Projects/ KPPIP	
	LRT Palembang	South Sumatra	USD755m[176]	Completed (operational)	Green	KPPPIP	
	Soekarno Hatta International Airport Express Train	Jakarta – Banten	USD1.7bn (IDR24.5tn)	Completed	Green	Priority project/ KPPIP	
	Makassar – Pare Pare Railway	South Sulawesi	USD574m (IDR8.2tn)	Under construction	Green	Priority project/ KPPIP	
	Rantau Prapat – Duri – Pekanbaru Railway	Jambi, Sumatra	USD721m (IDR10.3tn)	Under construction	Green	National Strategic Projects/ KPPIP	
	Kulon Progo Airport Access Railway	Yogyakarta	USD84m (IDR1.2tn)	Completed	Green	National Strategic Projects/ KPPIP	

Setor	Project name	Location	Cost (USD)	Status	Greenness	Pipeline source	Notes
Green Project (Continued)							
Low carbon transport	Medan-Binjai-Deli Serdang (Mebidang) LRT	Medan, North Sumatra	USD1.42bn (IDR20.3tn)[177]	Planned	Green	Others	
	Siantar – Parapat Railway	Medan, North Sumatra	USD847m (IDR12.1tn)[178]	Planned	Green	Others	
Renewable energy	**Hydropower**						
	Pelosika Dam Construction Project (2 x 10.5MW)	Southeast Sulawesi Province	USD600m	Planned	Potentially green	RPJMN 2020 – 2024	Seeking USD150 loan
	Peusangan 1 & 2 (87 MW)	Aceh Province, Sumatra	USD140m	Under construction	Potentially green	RPJMN 2020 – 2024	Seeking USD131m loan
	Matenggeng Pumped Storage Hydroelectric (4 x 225)	Central and West Java Province	USD1.04bn	Under construction	Potentially green	RPJMN 2020 – 2024	Seeking USD829.9 loan
	Karian Dam	Tangerang, Banten Province	USD88m	Under construction	Potentially green	RPJMN 2020 – 2024	Seeking USD50m loan
	Riam Kiwa Dam Construction Project	South Kalimantan Province	USD294.12m	Planned	Potentially green	RPJMN 2020 – 2024	Seeking a USD250m loan
	Upper Cisokan Pumped Storage Hydroelectric Plant (1040MW)	Bandung, West Java Province	USD910m	Planned	Potentially green	RPJMN 2020 – 2024	Seeking a USD650m loan
	Geothermal						
	Hululais 1 & 2 (55 MW x 2)	Bengkulu Province, Sumatra	USD246m	Under construction	Green	RPJMN 2020 – 2024	Seeking USD204m loan
	Blawan Ijen Geothermal Power Plant (110 MW)	Ijen, East Java	USD203m	Under construction	Green	PT SMI pipeline	
	Sarulla Geothermal Plant (330MW)	North Tapanuli, North Sumatra Province	USD1.17bn[179]	Completed	Green	Others	
	Solar						
	Ombilin Ground-mounted Solar PV (200MW)	West Sumatra	USD138.6m (IDR2tn, estimate)[180]	Planning	Green	Others	
	Tanjung Enim Ground-mounted Solar PV (200MW)	South Sumatra	USD138.6m (IDR2tn, estimate)[181]	Planning	Green	Others	
	Labuan Bajo Ground-mounted Solar PV (70 MW)	Labuan Bajo, East Nusa Tenggara	USD70m[182]	Planned	Green	Others	
	Biomass						
	Merauke Biomass Plant (3.5MW)	Merauke, Papua	USD9.7m (IDR140bn)	Completed	Green	Others	
	Wind						
	Tolo Jeneponton Wind Power Plant I (60 MW)	Jeneponton, South Sulawesi	USD154m (IDR2.2tn)	Completed	Green	Others	

Setor	Project name	Location	Cost (USD)	Status	Greenness	Pipeline source	Notes
Sustainable water management	Wosusokas Regional Water Supply System	Central Java Province	USD152m (IDR2.2tn)[183]	Planned	Potentially green	RPJMN 2020 – 2024, PPP Book 2021	Seeking USD95m loan
	Lambakan Dam Construction Project	East Kalimantan Province	USD647m	Planned	Potentially green	RPJMN 2020 – 2024	Seeking USD550m loan
	Water Resources Development in the Eastern Semarang and Upgrade of the Kedung Ombo Dam	Central Java Province	USD104m	Under construction	Potentially green	RPJMN 2020 – 2024	Seeking USD100m loan
	Jenelata Dam Construction Project	Gowa, South Sulawesi Province	USD352.4m	Planned	Potentially green	RPJMN 2020 – 2024	Seeking USD300m loan
	Karian Dam-Serpong Water Conveyance System	Banten and Jakarta Province	USD500.88m	Planned	Potentially green	RPJMN 2020 – 2024	Seeking USD402.78m loan
	Merangin Dam (107MW)	Jambi and West Sumatra Province	USD261m (IDR3.73tn)[184]	Planned	Potentially green	PPP Book 2021	
	Kamijoro Water Supply Project	Jogjakarta Special Region	USD24.3m (IDR347bn)[185]	Planning	Potentially green	RPJMN 2020 – 2024, PPP Book 2021	
	Lampung Water Supply Project	Bandar Lampung	USD82.6m[186]	Under construction	Potentially green	PPP Book 2021	
	Pekanbaru City Water Supply	Pekanbaru, Riau	USD51.45m IDR735bn[187]	Planned	Potentially green	PPP Book 2021	
	Flood Management and Coastal Protection Project	Coastlines of North Java	USD605m	Planned	Green	RPJMN 2020 – 2024	Seeking USD50m loan
Sustainable waste management	Sunter WtE Jakarta	Jakarta	USD400m	Planned	Potentially green		
	Bantar Gebang Refused Derifed Fueal Plant	Jakarta	USD105m (IDR1.5tn)	Planned	Potentially green	Jakarta City Government	Market sounding
	Cipeucang Waste to Energy Plant	South Tangerang, Banten Province	USD125.5m	Planned	Potentially green		
	WtE South Tangerang	South Tangerang, Banten	USD124m[188]	Planned	Potentially green	PPP Book 2021	
	WtE Bekasi (9 MW)	Bekasi, West Java	USD120m	Planned	Potentially green		
	WtE Bandung (29 MW)	Bandung, West Java	USD245m	Planned	Potentially green		
	Jatibarang WtE Plant	Semarang, Central Java	USD224m (IDR3.2tn)	Planned	Potentially green	Jakarta City Government, PPP Book 2021	Pre-feasibility study stage

Setor	Project name	Location	Cost (USD)	Status	Greenness	Pipeline source	Notes
Sustainable waste management	WtE Surakarta (10 MW)	Surakarta, Central Java	USD23m	Planned	Potentially green		
	WtE Surabaya - biomass	Surabaya, East Java	USD49.86m	Planned	Potentially green		
	WtE Makassar	Makassar, South Sulawesi	USD20m	Planned	Potentially green		
	WTE Denpasar	Denpasar, Bali	USD20m	Planned	Potentially green		
	WTE Palembang (20 MW)	Palembang, South Sumatera	USD260m (IDR1.8tn)	Planned	Potentially green		
	WTE Manado	Manado, North Sulawesi	USD20m	Planned	Potentially green		

Endnotes

1. Climate Bonds Initiative. 2019. Green Infrastructure Investment Opportunities (GIIO) Programme. https://www.climatebonds.net/green-infrastructure-investment-opportunities-giio-programme
2. ADB. 2017. Meeting Asia's Infrastructure Needs. Manila. February. https://www.adb.org/publications/asia-infrastructure-needs.
3. ADB. 2021. Partners Pledge $665 Million to Support Green Recovery in ASEAN. 2 November. https://www.adb.org/news/partners-pledge-665-million-support-green-recovery-asean
4. BKPM TV–Invest Indonesia. 2022. Transisi ke Ekonomi Hijau/What Have We Done and Ways Forward. YouTube webinar.
. Climate Bonds Initiative Green, Social and Sustainability Bonds Database (accessed October 2021).
6. Antara News. 2021. President encourages shift towards new. renewable energy. 16 August.
7. L. Sembiring. 2021. Sri Mulyani Bongkar Ada yang Lebih Mengerikan dari COVID-19. CNBC News (Indonesia edition). 28 July.
8. Government of Indonesia, Office of President. 2021. President Beberkan Tiga Strategi Besar Ekonomi Pada Ekonom. Jakarta.
9. Government of Indonesia, Ministry of Finance. 2019. http://www.data-apbn.kemenkeu.go.id/, Government of Indonesia, Ministry of Finance. 2021. Informasi APBN Kita 2021. Jakarta. (Accessed January 2021)
10. Cahya Puteri Abdi Rabbi. 2022. Belanja Infrastruktur Cetak Rekor Terbesar Rp 402 Triliun. Katadata. 5 January.
11. R. Van Doorn et al. 2020. Indonesia Public Expenditure Review 2020: Spending for Better Results. Washington, D.C.: World Bank Group.
12. IMD. 2020. IMD World Competitiveness Ranking 2020, H. Fajira. 2020. University of Indonesia News. LM FEB UI Announces Indonesia's Competitiveness 2020. 8 November.
13. IDN Financials. 2020. Bappenas estimates losses due to Greater Jakarta floods at Rp 5,2 trillion. 2 January.
14. Mercy Corps Indonesia. 2021. Technical Working Report: Climate Risk and Impact Assessment of Pekalongan, Indonesia.
15. Mercy Corps Indonesia. 2021. Technical Working Report: Climate Risk and Impact Assessment of Pekalongan, Indonesia.
16. ADB and World Bank. 2021. Climate Risk Profile: Indonesia (2021).
17. Indonesian Central Statistics Agency. 2021. Ekonomi Indonesia 2020 turun sebesar 2-07 persen c to c. (accessed January 2022).
18. Indonesian Central Statistics Agency. 2021. Februari 2021: Tingkat Pengangguran Terbuka (TPT) sebesar 6,26 persen (accessed January 2022); IDX Channel. 2020. Dua Juta Lebih Penduduk Kehilangan Pekerjaan Akibat COVID-19, 2020.
19. Indonesian Central Statistics Agency. 2021. Persentase Penduduk Miskin Maret 2021 turun menjadi 10,14 persen, 2021 (accessed January 2022).
20. UNICEF, UNDP, Prospera, and SMERU. 2021. Analysis of the Social and Economic Impacts of COVID-19 on Households and Strategic Policy Recommendations for Indonesia, 2021.
21. Government of Indonesia, Cabinet Secretariat. 2021. Finance Minister Reveals 2022 State Budget Bill Focus for Health Sector. 25 August; Government of Indonesia, Ministry of Finance. State Budget 2021. Jakarta.
22. Asian Development Bank (ADB). 2021. Asian Development Outlook 2021 Update.
23. Government of Indonesia, Ministry of Finance. 2021. Fiscal and Economic Updates, July 2021. Jakarta.
24. Government of Indonesia, Minister of Finance. 2021. Speech, Sri Mulyani Indrawati. October; Antara News. 2021. Climate change impact as devastating as COVID-19 pandemic: minister.
25. Climate Policy Initiative. 2021. Improving the impact of fiscal stimulus in Asia: An analysis of green recovery investments and opportunities.
26. ADB. 2021. ADB Briefs: Implementing a Green Recovery in Southeast Asia. Manila.
27. International Finance Corporation (IFC). 2021. A Green Reboot for Emerging Markets.
28. Financial Stability Board. 2020. The Implications of Climate Change for Financial Stability.

29. International Finance Corporation (IFC). 2021. A Green Reboot for Emerging Markets.
30. World Bank, Indonesia. 2021. Indonesia Economic Prospects (IEP), June 2021: Boosting the recovery. Jakarta.
31. Government of Indonesia, Ministry of National Development Planning (BAPPENAS). 2020. Rencana Pembangunan Jangka Menengah Nasional (RPJMN) 2020- 2024. Jakarta; T. Pangastuti. 2021. Pemerintah Hanya Mampu Danai Pembangunan Infrastruktur 37% Target RPJMN. Investor ID. 8 July.
32. Government of Indonesia, Ministry of Finance. 2021. Updated Nationally Determined Contribution 2021.
33. Government of Indonesia, Ministry of Finance. 2021. Transformasi Ekonomi Hijau untuk Masa Depan Peradaban. Jakarta.
34. G. Iacurci. 2021. Money invested in ESG funds more than doubles in a year. CNBC. 11 February.
35. AIIB. 2020. Mobilizing Finance: Recent Trends and Giving a Stronger Push Toward Sustainable Investment. Asian Infrastructure Finance. 16 April. pp. 58–65.
36. Climate Bonds Initiative. 2021. ASEAN Sustainable Finance State of the Market 2020.
37. Climate Bonds Initiative. Green Sukuk. (accessed January 2022).
38. Ministry of Finance, Interview with the Director of Syariah Financing, Dwi Irianti Hadiningdyah. November 2021.
39. N. Harsono. 2020. ADB, PLN to pilot issuance of energy transition bonds in 2021. Jakarta Post. 3 November; A. Richter. 2021. Indonesian PT Pertamina eyes green bond issuance by 2022. Think Geoenergy. 10 April.
40. Otoritas Jasa Keuangan (OJK). 2020. SURAT EDARAN OTORITAS JASA KEUANGAN NOMOR .../SEOJK.04/2020.
41. PT SMI. 2021. Interview. 18 November.
42. PT SMI. 2021. Interview. 18 November.
43. Climate Bonds Initiative. 2019. Unlocking green bonds in Indonesia: a guide for issuers, regulators and investors.
44. Climate Bonds Initiative. 2019. Unlocking green bonds in Indonesia: a guide for issuers, regulators and investors.
45. Government of Singapore, Monetary Authority of Singapore. 2020. MAS Launches World's First Grant Scheme to Support Green and Sustainability-Linked Loans. Singapore.
46. Forbes. 2019. Why ESG Matters Among Wealthy Investors. 7 November.
47. Wing-Far Cheng. 2012. Asia is a long-term investment for global pension funds. IPE Magazine. November.
48. Climate Bonds Initiative. 2021. ASEAN Sustainable Finance State of the Market 2020.
49. Climate Bonds Initiative Green, Social and Sustainability Bonds Database (accessed January 2022).
50. Ministry of National Economic Development and Planning (BAPPENAS). Low Carbon Develoment: A Paradigm Shift Towards A Green Economy in Indonesia. 2019.
51. A. Muhammad. 2021. Indonesia Targetkan Net Zero 2060. IDX Channel. https://www.idxchannel.com/economics/indonesia-targetkan-net-zero-2060; Video exclusive. 2021. Tanpa Investor, Pensiun PLTU Baru Terealisasi di 2056. CNBC Indonesia. 29 November.
52. ADB. 2021. Energy Transition Mechanism Explainer: How ETM Will Support Climate Action in Southeast Asia. News Release. 3 November.
53. Indonesia Financial Service Authority (OJK). Otoritas Jasa Keuangan Regulation No. 51, in 2017 (POJK). 2017.
54. DIPPR CBI. 2021. Interview.
55.
56.
57. N. Harsono. 2020. ADB, PLN to pilot issuance of energy transition bonds in 2021. Jakarta Post. 3 November; A. Richter. 2021. Indonesian PT Pertamina eyes green bond issuance by 2022. Think Geoenergy. 10 April.
58. Perusahaan Listrik Negara (PLN). 2021. PLN Statement of Intent on Sustainable Financing Framework.

59. Climate Policy Initiative. 2021. Municipal green bonds crucial to unlocking renewable energy financing. 15 July.
60. W. Yahya and P. Dirgahayani. 2020. Mapping of the governance problem in the implementation of an unsolicited public-private partnership project (the case of Jatiluhur regional water supply phase i). IOP Conf. Ser.: Earth Environ. Sci. 592 012019; ADB. 2019. Renewable energy financing schemes for Indonesia.
61. Climate Bonds Initiative. 2019. Unlocking green bonds in Indonesia: a guide for issuers, regulators and investors.
62. Climate Bonds Initiative. 2019. Unlocking green bonds in Indonesia: a guide for issuers, regulators and investors.
63. Climate Bonds Initiative. 2019. ASEAN Green Financial Instruments Guide.
64. IFC. 2018. IFC Invests in Bank OCBC NISP for Pioneering Green Bond. Press release. 1 August.
65. Climate Bonds Initiative. 2019. ASEAN Green Financial Instruments Guide.
66. OECD. 2021. De-risking institutional investments in green infrastructure; Inter-American Development Bank (IADB). 2018. Multilateral Banks Risk Mitigation Instruments for Infrastructure Investments.
67. ADB. 2017. DFI Working Group on Blended Concessional Finance for Private Sector Projects. Manila; World Bank. 2020. What is blended finance, and how can it help deliver successful high-impact, high-risk projects?; OECD. Blended Finance Principles.
68. Climate Bonds Initiative. 2019. ASEAN Green Financial Instruments Guide.
69. ADB. 2019. New Facility to Mobilise USD1bn for ASEAN Green Infrastructure. News Release. 4 April; ADB. 2020. ACGF Overview. Manila.
70. ADB. 2020. Indonesia: Sustainable Development Goals Indonesia One - Green Finance Facility (Phase 1). Manila.
71. PT Sarana Multi Infrastruktur. 2021. SDG Indonesia One – Pencapaian dan Rencana Kerja. Power-point Presentation. October. (Accessed January 2022)
72. PT Sarana Multi Infrastruktur. 2021. SDG Indonesia One – Pencapaian dan Rencana Kerja. Power-point Presentation. October. (Accessed January 2022)
73. PT Sarana Multi Infrastruktur. 2021. SDG Indonesia One – Pencapaian dan Rencana Kerja. Power-point Presentation. October. . (Accessed January 2022)
74. ADB. ACGF Overview. Manila.
75. ADB. 2020. Proposed Loan and Technical Assistance Grant Indonesia: Sustainable Development Goals Indonesia One – Green Finance Facility Phase 1. Manila.
76. ADB. 2020. Green Finance Strategies for Post-COVID-19 Econo3mic Recovery in Southeast Asia. Manila.
77. ADB. 2020. Green Finance Strategies for Post-COVID-19 Economic Recovery in Southeast Asia. Manila.
78. ADB. 2021. Interview with Anouj Mehta, ACGF, ADB. 18 November.
79. ADB. 2021. Partners Pledge USD665 Million to Support Green Recovery in ASEAN. News release. 2 November.
80. Project Drawdown (n/a). Electricity Generation Geothermal. Retrieved from https://www.drawdown.org/solutions/electricity-generation/geothermal
81. International Energy Agency (2019). Hydropower. Retrieved from https://www.iea.org/fuels-and-technologies/hydropower
82. UNFCCC (2018). Clean Energy Transition Needs to Accelerate. Retrieved from https://unfccc.int/news/clean-energy-transition-needs-to-accelerate
83. UNFCCC (2016). Railway Sector on Track to Acheive Low Carbon Goals. Retrieved from https://unfccc.int/news/railway-sector-on-track-to-acheive-low-carbon-goals
84. UNFCCC (2015). World Needs to Manage Water more sustainably. Retrieved from https://unfccc.int/news/world-needs-to-manage-water-more-sustainably

www.ingramcontent.com/pod-product-compliance
Lightning Source LLC
Chambersburg PA
CBHW041622220326

41599CB00043BA/7223